D0792617

CITIES OF LIGHT

What Communities Can Accomplish in the New Age

Swami Kriyananda (J. Donald Walters)

CITIES OF LIGHT

What Communities Can Accomplish in the New Age

Swami Kriyananda

Crystal Clarity Publishers
Nevada City, California

Crystal Clarity Publishers
14618 Tyler Foote Road
Nevada City, CA 95959-8599
800.424.1055
530.478.7600
fax: 530.478.7610
clarity@crystalclarity.com
Web site: www.crystalclarity.com

Library of Congress Cataloging-in-Publication Data

Walters, J. Donald.
  Cities of light : what communities can accomplish in the New Age /
Swami Kriyananda.
      p. cm.
  Includes index.
  ISBN 1-56589-172-4 (trade paper)
  1. Ananda Cooperative Village. 2. Community. 3. Cooperativeness. I.
Title.
  BP605.S38A52 2004
  299'.93--dc22
                                              2004020792

This book is dedicated
to all who seek crystal clarity
in their daily lives, in their associations with others,
in their work, and in self-understanding.

Crystal Clarity

A New Concept in Living

Crystal Clarity means to see oneself, and all things, as aspects of a greater reality; to seek to enter into conscious attunement with that reality; and to see all things as channels for the expression of that reality.

It means to see truth in simplicity; to seek always to be guided by the simple truth, not by opinion; and by what *is*, not by one's own desires or prejudices.

It means striving to see things in relation to their broadest potential.

In one's association with other people, it means seeking always to include their realities in one's own.

Contents

Foreword

This book starts with a noble dream: "Imagine a beautiful city. . . ." Reading these first lines, you might think impatiently: "Well, here comes another dreamer. . . ."

Far from it, dear reader! *Cities of Light* is not "wishful thinking" at all, not a beautiful castle in the clouds, which by tomorrow is already forgotten! Swami Kriyananda proposes and lives for high ideals, oh yes. But the greatness of *Cities of Light* lies in its practicality. It is grounded in profound knowledge of human nature, an insight the author has gained from a lifetime of guiding people. Kriyananda's lifelong question concerning his communitarian ideal has been: "Does it work?"

And yes, it does work! You will read about an existing community, Ananda, which has been around happily for thirty-five years. Sometimes the author jokingly says: "I think Ananda is the best-kept secret around." Only few know about it, beautiful though it is. I myself have lived in an Ananda community in Italy, called Ananda Assisi, for the last fourteen years. And it is with greatest joy that I announce here (I wish a book could have a microphone and a loudspeaker!): "Yes, friends, it really does work. It is wonderful! It will never be perfect, that's for sure. But a better life *is* possible! I have seen it! Ananda is a living testimony. People from many countries live here in beautiful harmony as I have not seen elsewhere during my many years of travel. I am most grateful to be here and wish many more people could live this way."

Cities of Light, however, is not really about one specific place. It is about high principles which can be applied by everyone who is willing to try—wherever he lives, whatever his creed, culture, or social background may be.

In *Cities of Light*, Swami Kriyananda introduces a central concept that he calls "Crystal Clarity." He goes on to apply this concept to all facets of our life. He asks: What does it mean to live high ideals in relationships, in business, in marriage, in education, in government? And how can I, the reader, contribute to bringing these high principles down to earth? For people wanting to live together with high ideals, Swami Kriyananda asks: Which principles will make a community work in a successful and fulfilling way?

The principles discussed in *Cities of Light* deserve to be studied carefully. They carry within themselves the seeds to transform our lives. More than that, they are a workable key to revolutionize our society, to bring it to a higher octave: not from without, by imposing a new political system onto people, but from within, from the people themselves, from new convictions and perceptions, from a new ideal.

Of course each new development needs its "Pilgrim Fathers." It always begins on a small scale, with those pioneers who are ready to walk the first steps. And so, dear reader, *Cities of Light* is an invitation for you to be such a person, carrying for others the torch-light of a wonderful future!

Our hope is that this book will bear plentiful fruit. May it help in bringing about a new era, a new way of life, a new and better society—radiant with harmony, true friendship, and lasting peace.

Jayadev Jaerschky

Cities of Tomorrow

Chapter one

Imagine a city—a beautiful city, such as a City of Tomorrow ought to be.

Imagine small residential areas within the city, each surrounded by beautiful parkland for its residents' enjoyment.

Imagine homes joyfully designed according to their residents' needs, their outlook on life, their tastes, the way they relate to the land around them. Imagine each home, therefore, a *conscious* home.

Imagine beautiful, expansive vistas wherever you feast your eyes—distant hills and valleys, nearby meadows, trees, and flowers.

Imagine a city in which the residents really have a say in determining its shape, its growth, its overall philosophy, development, and design.

Imagine farm and dairy land not struggling for lonely, competitive survival, but ownership of them shared by all, and a vital part of the life of everyone.

Imagine shops where the keynote is friendship; where the salespeople think in terms of giving to the customers instead of taking from them.

Imagine shops where the salespeople are the owners, and have a vital interest in the shops' success.

Imagine businesses where the workers' personal needs outweigh the businesses' quest for income: a place where *people are more important than things.*

Imagine a community of people who know how to cooperate joyfully together, with kindness in their hearts for one another, and for all those whom their lives touch.

Imagine a community where the leadership is supportive, not bossy; where the emphasis in leadership is on serving, not on ruling.

Imagine a city where, when someone needs help, everyone freely and lovingly joins in helping him.

Imagine a city where human values are given first importance, and where the desire for joy and harmony and love are looked upon as needs every bit as practical as material considerations.

Imagine a city that doesn't place self-interest first, but that takes into account its impact on the well-being of society at large, and adjusts its expectations to that greater good.

Imagine a city that seeks no help from federal, state, or county government; a city whose inhabitants think, instead, how they might serve the good of the greater nation.

Imagine a city with schools that teach children the art of living, along with the standard offerings of academia; schools that teach them the meaning of success in human, and not in merely economic, terms; schools that teach them how to attract success, how to concentrate, how to overcome their negative moods, how to get along with others.

Imagine schools that seek, along with their formal curriculum, to teach students how to be happy!

Imagine a city ruled by a conscious quest for happiness and peace of mind, and not by economic greed; a city without crime; a city where good will and honesty are taken for granted.

Imagine a place where community meetings are always harmonious; where people view the good of all as more important than their own desires. Imagine community forums where everyone wants, and expects, the decisions to be based on truth, not on opinion; on what is right, not on what is merely desired (whether by one person, or by the whole community). Imagine people with different views deferring to one another, conceding points, cheerfully admitting errors—and in the end all agreeing harmoniously on a course of action.

Imagine a creative life, where people's goal is to improve their understanding; a city whose residents offer one another help constructively, compassionately, and not by confrontation, in their efforts to improve themselves.

Imagine a place where self-improvement is not approached with tension or with an attitude of guilt, but joyfully, serenely, with the understanding that neither guilt nor tension ever helped a tree to grow.

Imagine a place where people *live* to find joy and inspiration, and where they want to share their inspiration with others; a place where "getting ahead in life" is understood in terms of inner, self-development.

Imagine a life based on a search for inner, Crystal Clarity of mind and heart—a place where people seek to express that clarity in their work, in their home environment, in the arts, in home building, in teaching, in their lives and their relationships.

Imagine a City of Light. Here, the light sought is not material, merely, but is sought first in terms of expanded understanding and awareness.

Imagine a place where people's hearts are simple, without selfish motive; where the residents sincerely love truth and God, and strive to see God equally in all mankind.

"Such a place," perhaps you'll say, "may be imaginable. But is it *possible*?"

It *is* possible, for such a place exists! Its reality, moreover, suggests amazing possibilities for modern mankind. The experiment has been conducted long enough to have earned the right to make this very simple claim: *It works!*

The first land for the experiment was purchased in 1967. The initial buildings were completed in 1968. Slowly, through nearly twenty years, the experiment has developed, always testing the vision by the yardstick of proved reality.

Almost everything in the above description matches present reality. This is no affirmation, merely, but fact. The only part of the above description that remains to be realized—and it is sure to be fulfilled in time—is that of the parkland surrounding the clusters of homes. The homes are there—simple, lovely residences. The land around them is there also. This land, however, though parklike in its beauty, still lacks the gardener's careful touch.

The other parts of the above description, however—the harmony, the compassion, the sharing character of the residents, the primary purpose for the businesses, the physical beauty of the land and of the homes, the all-pervasive sense of happiness—all that I've written, in fact, describes the place as it actually is, and not as the residents hope that it will become someday.

It is not a city. Even so, several hundred deeply involved residents is a noteworthy beginning. There is no reason, moreover, on the basis of developments to date, that cities could not spring up across America, inspired by this vision of light, and founded by people who feel, without rejection of their fellow man, that dark greed and self-centered competitiveness simply will not work.

The community now in existence is called Ananda World Brotherhood Village. It is a prototype, an offering to others who may feel inspired to build on this example in their own way.

"Large oaks from little acorns grow." What has been accomplished so far is a reality. It remains a dream also, however, in the sense that, from these beginnings, others may create villages, towns, and Cities of Light across the land— communities based on cooperation and friendship, high ideals, simple living, truth, and love for God.

Ananda World Brotherhood Village is situated in the Sierra Nevada foothills of northern California. It has several branch communities—in Palo Alto, San Francisco, and Sacramento, California; in Seattle, Washington; and near Assisi, Italy. It also has many groups of friends who strive to live in Crystal Clarity according to the principles on which Ananda was founded.

The purpose of this book, however, is to interest the reader in a set of practical ideals, not in a mere physical location. Ananda will be referred to repeatedly as a living example of these ideals. The emphasis, however, will be on what others can do to create, partly on the strength of this example, more harmonious environments for themselves.

May the day come when people everywhere realize that it is possible for them to live in joy and harmony, and that the cities they construct verily *can* become Cities of Light!

To Get What You Want, Clarify Your Goals

Chapter two

"If this idea is so worthwhile, why hasn't it been tried before?"

The question is inevitable. There are two answers to it. First, the idea *has* been tried, repeatedly, and sometimes successfully. Heretofore, however, it has not been tried in such a way as to offer a viable model to other groups.

The second answer is more important, and can be summed up in a single word: *habit*. History so far shows people coming together for basically one reason only: economics. There may be a convenient harbor, so commerce flourishes, and a city springs into existence to promote that commerce. Or there may be a mine, and men flock there to work. A community develops out of their need to live, shop, and find their recreation nearby. Or it may be that a town grows up around a large factory.

The economic motive is taken so much for granted that people rarely question the possibility of other motives. Yet surely there are many who have wished, if only fleetingly, that their lives could be centered in some higher vision; that they could have neighbors who shared that vision, and who were close friends—people with whom they could interact in harmony and happiness.

There is a growing need for an alternative. The shrugging off of higher values that has been the hallmark of the Twentieth Century is causing a reaction in many people. They are beginning to want to center their lives more consciously in God. Their souls reject the claim of the social philosophies of today that man is merely a "social animal."

A change of lifestyle is not so difficult to achieve as most people think. All that is required is that people change their mental attitudes. Such transformations are a daily phenomenon in the lives of individuals. Why not coordinated change by large groups of individuals?

"People can't be expected to change their attitudes!" One hears the dogma constantly as an excuse for rejecting change. The thought, indeed, seems deeply embedded in human consciousness.

What, then, will these devotees of convention make of Ananda? Attitudes, here at Ananda, quite simply *have* been changed! We are dealing with facts, not theories. Hundreds of people in America and abroad have changed their attitudes so radically that they've given up well-paying jobs, success, and high positions to join a community that offered them something infinitely more precious than any worldly goal: happiness.

It would be a mistake, moreover, to see in this fact anything unprecedented. History shows us many periods when whole movements developed because large numbers of people simply changed their minds about how things ought to be done. There is no good reason to insist that such changes are impossible today. They have occurred repeatedly, and under many varied circumstances. Some of these great movements involved embracing lives of total self-denial, that sincere men and women might live their lives more perfectly for God.

Today, total renunciation is not what is being asked of mankind. The present need is for a life of dedication, yes, but in simplicity, not in poverty; in creative self-expression, not in unthinking submission and obedience.

How can people be inspired to give up their natural ego-centeredness? To do so would seem to flout one of the fundamentals of human nature. The solution is simple: Don't ask them to give up egoism, but only to define their ego-fulfillments more broadly.

For example: Once the good of others is honestly seen as more conducive to personal happiness than grabbing whatever one can for oneself, it becomes relatively easy to include their happiness in one's own.

At Ananda, we have found that even the most all-pervasive human tendencies can be redirected, given a strong enough motive. Why, for example, live for God rather than for self-gratification? Simply because God's love and joy are infinitely *more* gratifying!

What prevents people from living in such a way that they can have everything in life they really want? Habit, quite simply. Most people aren't even accustomed to giving a conscious direction to their lives. They live haphazardly. They take jobs merely because the jobs happen to be there, and available, not because the jobs themselves hold any special fascination for them. They buy homes because the price is right, not because they like, or even know, the neighbors. They marry for the convenience of having a companion, not often because of any deep affinity with the person they select. They drift through life like petals on a stream, acted upon more often than acting.

Such people seldom bring about deliberately anything that happens in their lives. They are effects, merely; the cause for whatever happens to them lies indifferently at a distance, far beyond their control.

Thus, they find themselves motivated entirely by obvious needs: food, clothing, and shelter. A typical statement by many social "scientists" in this century has been, "If you give a person food, clothing, and shelter, he will have everything he wants." This teaching may seem true in a society where people haven't enough of any of these. It becomes a travesty of human need, however, when pushed to the extreme of what is euphemistically called "consumerism."

Mankind cannot remain satisfied forever with things that feed his body, but not his mind or soul. If he lives consciously at all, the acquisition of a roof over his head, enough clothing to keep him warm, and food to sustain his body merely free him to pursue deeper and more natural interests. For man is no mere biological machine. He has mental, emotional, and spiritual needs that can never be satisfied at the supermarket.

How many popular songs have echoed back to us reminders of what we all know in our hearts to be true: that love and happiness can't be bought; that material success means nothing if, in the act of seeking it, we lose our peace of mind.

An artist, in order to get a sense of proportion in his work, steps back from his canvas. People ought to do the same, periodically, with their lives. It is important for us to take charge of our lives. What is the point of drifting heedlessly wherever life's currents may see fit to carry us? As much as possible, we should try to control our destinies.

Stepping back a little, then, from the canvas we've been painting of our lives—or perhaps merely observing while it gets painted for us—let us ask ourselves, "What do I really want from my life?"

Is it money? If so, what do we want it for?

Is it prestige? Again, what for?

Is it "to get ahead"? What does it really mean, "to get ahead"?

Always, the answer, when we dive down deep enough beneath the surface of present crises and ambitions, is to avoid pain, and to find happiness. It's really quite that simple!

We identify pain with specific things, such as an insufficiency of money, ill health, or loss of a job. And we identify happiness with the opposites of these things: sufficient money, good health, a good job.

A survey was made several years ago which asked people if they were happy with their present incomes. The majority, regardless of how much or how little money they earned, replied, "I'd be happy if I could only earn 10% more."

That 10% is the carrot on the stick, inviting the donkey to keep walking, and so to keep on dragging his cartload of worries behind him!

Pain and happiness are mental states; they are not things. As popular wisdom itself says, all the money in the world can't protect us from suffering, and all the money in the world can't buy us happiness.

Happiness is not something we derive from things. Money, power, a beautiful home—none of these can give it to us. This inner, mental state should be made the primary goal in our lives. At present, it is, for almost all people, their secondary goal—a goal they hope to attain *as a result of* some other achievement.

The usual question asked when setting out in life should be changed from, "How do I earn enough money to be happy?" to, "What are the conditions for happiness?" Only then will people be ready to ask the second question: "How can I sustain those conditions?"

One of the lessons that have been learned at Ananda over the years is that those people are happy who give and share with others. The opposite has proved true also: Those people are unhappy who think first of themselves. Observing the examples of hundreds of members, not all of whom have made the best choices in their lives, the message has become crystal clear. What it involves is a simple, basic law of human nature.

Jesus put it succinctly when he said, "It is more blessed to give than to receive,"—"blessed," because blissful. The ego feels cramped by its own selfishness. Our normal human desire, always, is to expand our self-identity. But when people seek their self-expansion by accumulation, they succeed only in reinforcing the walls confining them.

People find happiness in sharing with others; in living for high ideals; in living more simply; above all, in living for God.

Given any kind of ideals at all, isn't it a source of joy to be able to share creatively with others who share those ideals? Wouldn't one's place of residence, then, ideally be among such true friends, and not merely in some location where the price happened to be right?

Wouldn't it be wonderful to work with people of like mind, and not only with people who were employed because, like you, they answered a want ad?

Wouldn't it be wonderful to work under people, also, who had your interests sincerely at heart; who didn't view you only in terms of your economic value to the firm?

Wouldn't it be wonderful to have friends with whom you could cry, and not only acquaintances with whom you laughed superficially at patio parties? Wouldn't it be wonderful, in fact, to have friends with whom you could share, joyfully, your deepest interests and concerns? And wouldn't it be wonderful to have friends who remained loyal to you, no matter whether Fortune smiled or frowned on you?

The solution is so simple: Seek these less substantial-seeming, but infinitely more rewarding, values first, not last!

Jesus urged people to "Seek the kingdom of God first, and all these things shall be added unto you." The principle applies equally today.

The more a person lives by high principles, the more he will find everything else in his life falling naturally into place. The more, however, he tries with both hands and both feet to hold everything in place, hoping that inner happiness will come of itself, the less he finds himself in control of anything, and the more he finds his dreams of happiness, peace of mind, and God receding before his gaze.

People become as if hypnotized by habit. Tell them, "Let's find a way to put happiness first in our lives," and their immediate, because ever-conditioned, response is, "But how will we support ourselves?" Their "but" is as much as to say that their thoughts have reverted instantly to the old question, and with it the old pursuit, "How will we support ourselves?"

When seeking new solutions to any problem, the best course is to concentrate on finding the solutions, and not to paralyze the search with problem-consciousness. The best method is first to give fresh possibilities an opportunity to acquire self-definition.

To find a right solution, the first step is to ask the right questions. In a well worded question, in fact, the answer will be almost always clear already. Ask, then, the question, "How can I find happiness in my life?" The answer almost writes itself: By putting happiness first, and not seeking it merely incidentally.

"When am I happiest?" Search your own life, and you'll surely find the answer: "When I live for higher values, and when I share that higher life with others."

The first thing to do, then, is seek some way to follow such a calling, and to interest others in living such a life with you. Once the vision is crystal clear in the minds of all of you, the way to its manifestation will be found.

The early pioneering settlers of the Far West held to their dreams. Fortunately, they had no idea of the obstacles they would face in the fulfillment of those dreams, or most might have clung to the safety and comforts of home. Still, they dreamed, and out of their dreams was born the present, still-incredible reality.

The saying, "Where there's a will, there's a way," has been validated again and again in history. If your primary goal, deeply held, is happiness, you will, you *must*, find a way to pursue and support that goal.

You will never find happiness, however, if that is not your deliberate aim. For most people, this fundamental human right, "The pursuit of happiness," has come to signify instead, "The pursuit of property."

Creative action is always preceded by an idea. States of mind never evolve automatically out of material form, nor out of merely material activity.

Begin, therefore, with the question, "How much is happiness worth to me?" If the answer is, "Everything!" you are halfway already to a solution.

The members of Ananda frequently exclaim to one another, "How did such a wonderful thing as this ever happen to us? Our friends in the cities often earn more than we do, yet they haven't a fraction of what we have here! They live in little apartments, are forever in debt, quarrel with their neighbors or their landlords, have few, if any, close friends. Here at Ananda we have lovely homes, open space, beautiful scenery, wonderful friends, harmonious relationships, meaningful lives. We even get to take vacations more than many people do! If only we could get people to see that this is the only *possible* way to live!

"But," they then ask, "how did it all come about?"

They know the answer, of course. It's only that the sheer simplicity of this answer makes them still shake their heads in wonder.

The answer lies in *cooperation*. People who do things together, instead of each one battling alone, can move mountains. An Ananda saying puts it well: "Many hands make a miracle."

Years ago, during the Indo-Pakistani war, a friend of mine was riding on a bus in Pakistan. The bus driver, to avoid the Indian planes which were strafing the roads, took a detour. At one point he tried to ford a stream, and the bus got stuck in the mud. The driver asked the passengers to get out and push.

Fifteen minutes of hard pushing passed. Still the bus hadn't moved an inch. The driver at last stepped back to see what was wrong. To his dismay, he found half the passengers pushing with might and main from the rear, while the other half were pushing just as hard from the front!

So much human energy gets expended uselessly, when people think only of shifting for themselves. They work against one another, and even against themselves, without even realizing it. Their affirmations of self-interest conflict with the interests of others. Life for everyone becomes unceasing war.

If, then, you want to make the impossible happen, remember, the first key is clarity: Crystal Clarity. Once you know clearly what you want, you'll be halfway to a solution.

The second key is cooperation—willing, enthusiastic cooperation, never coerced, but offered voluntarily, with joy, because you deeply believe in what you're doing.

Living in Crystal Clarity

Chapter three

The delusion of communism has sprung out of perhaps the greatest error of our age: the belief that matter is the fundamental reality; and consciousness, only an illusory manifestation of that reality.

Organic and inorganic matter have been shown to have so many essential points in common that scientists now insist that both are aspects of one and the same reality. Materialists have drawn from this fact the conclusion that life, too, is fundamentally inanimate, and so also consciousness—since thought, and therefore consciousness, is comparable in every way to the mechanical functions of a computer.

Science itself, with its traditionally mechanistic bias, prompts people to this wholly materialistic conclusion.

If one steps back a little, however, from the obvious bias implicit here, it becomes immediately obvious that the opposite conclusion is every bit as logical: namely, that all matter is fundamentally animate and therefore conscious.

Religious dogma, strange to say, has steadfastly rejected this explanation. Perhaps theologians haven't yet faced up to the fact that a choice has been thrust upon them: namely, that either consciousness is material, or else matter is a manifestation of consciousness. For them, the second choice is a plum. It knocks head over heels every claim of materialism. Yet they refuse to choose. In fact, they insist that matter does not in any way manifest God's consciousness. And so they hand the game, set, and match to the materialists. In God's name, why?

Dogmas are not truths. They are human ideas about truth. Christian dogmas were formulated to meet the exigencies of early centuries. Those circumstances, however, never forced people to think things through quite as far as we're being forced to think them today. The scientific claim that consciousness is a material phenomenon cries out for the contrary claim, that matter is a phenomenon of consciousness—else all values are baseless, and life itself has no meaning.

Materialism has found its natural philosophy in communism. Communism is simply materialism trying to create for itself an aura of respectability. It might even be called the religion of materialism. In fact, it often *has* been called a pseudo-religion.

As long, therefore, as materialism remains such a widespread belief, intelligent people will continue to feel drawn, even against the dictates of their common sense, into the vortex of communistic philosophy. The reason is simply that communism expresses, inescapably, the logical consequences of their materialistic belief.

Communism holds that thought and consciousness are basically unreal, except as an electronic "manipulation of memory traces in the brain"—the sort of thing computers do even better than we can. The least thinking member of society, the manual laborer, is exalted under communism to the pinnacle of merit. Independent thought is both discouraged and persecuted. Idealism is ridiculed. Moral values are accepted as conveniences, merely, for the achievement of social ends. Lies are the accepted way of achieving those ends. Indeed, if a lie can advance the cause of communism, it is not considered a lie at all, but is the official communist definition of a truth.

The dogmas that are normally propounded in the churches are not adequate to conquer the opponents of religion in this struggle. It is therefore very important to understand that Christian dogma is not Christianity's last word on anything. Dogmas are man-made definitions—interpretations of revelation, rather than revelation itself. They were formulated to meet the needs and understanding of a former age.

Jesus, certainly, through his miracles, and when speaking of answered prayer, demonstrated clearly enough his belief that matter is both a lower reality than consciousness, and subject to the commands of consciousness. He said that by faith we can move mountains.

Indeed, if matter can be subjugated in any way to human consciousness, we see already a relationship implied between matter and consciousness. We have here, then, sufficient justification already for saying that consciousness, and not matter, *is* the reality; that all things material are not merely the creations of a distant God, but inherently divine, because manifestations of His ever-present consciousness.

This explanation takes us right back to the claim made in the last chapter, that the first step in anything one attempts is to formulate a clear *idea* of what it is one wants to accomplish. Crystal Clarity of consciousness, then, is the prerequisite for success in any undertaking.

Thus is faith justified as the most practical ingredient of success in any endeavor. A clear concept, projected with force of will onto outward reality, is capable of changing even matter according to the wishes of the mind.

If people want to create Cities of Light, their first step must be to visualize them clearly—not only as a possibility, but as a *reality* in both space and time, right here in America.

The first question should not be, "How shall we support ourselves?" Rather, it should be, "What is this high ideal? How shall we define it?" Later, once clarity on this level is achieved, people can take up the important second question, "How, then, shall we support this ideal?"

King Alfred the Great of England reached a point in his career when he seemed to have been vanquished by his foes, the Danes. There was virtually no one left to support him. He had been driven back, almost alone, to the fragile security of a little island. There he hid, his whereabouts unknown. Everyone thought his cause was lost. The Danes, relaxed now in victory, stopped thinking of him as a threat.

Alfred's clarity of purpose, however, never left him. Secretly he rounded up his supporters, and formed them into a striking force. At last, he attacked the unsuspecting enemy, and defeated them. Thus, he succeeded in winning back his throne, his kingdom, and, in the end, many years of peace for England.

We live today in a time of clear alternatives. *So clear are these alternatives, in fact, and so pressing are their claims upon us, that we have literally no alternative but to face them, and choose between them!* Never before have the choices confronting mankind been so clear. Because we *must* choose, the opportunities for inner growth at this time are enormous also. They may even be unprecedented.

On the one hand, we are faced with the descending darkness of materialism, and all that that implies: atheism, cynicism, want of any principle except the ultimately self-destructive goal of "getting mine."

On the other hand, we are faced with the ever-more-expansive vision of a universe wholly manifested out of God, and therefore inherently divine, and with a divine calling to unite our souls with God—a God who loves us, and who will love us through all eternity; a God who is our very own.

Clarity in this choice is being forced upon us. If we refuse to face it, or if we choose darkness instead of light, it is we ourselves who will have to suffer for our mistake. I might even say, it is ourselves whom, in a very real sense, we'll have rejected.

Today's need for clarity is broader even than one might suppose. For clarity defined as mere reason or common sense is not enough, and is a travesty of the potentials before us. Clarity, rightly understood, means opening up our entire being to a Higher Reality, that that Reality might penetrate not only our minds, but our feelings, our bodies, our intellects, our very souls.

When Jesus said, "Blessed are the pure in heart, for they shall see God," he was saying, in effect, "Blessed are those whose hearts are Crystal Clear, without blemish, capable of transmitting perfectly to the world the light they receive from within."

To live in Crystal Clarity means to see oneself, and all things, as aspects of a greater reality; to seek to enter into conscious attunement with that reality; and to see all things as channels for the expression of that reality.

It means to see truth in simplicity; to seek always to be guided by the simple truth, not by opinion; and by what IS, not by one's own desires or prejudices.

It means striving to see things in relation to their broadest potential.

In one's association with other people, it means seeking always to include their realities in one's own.

In the 1960s, hundreds of communities were started in a great "back-to-the-land" movement. Why did almost all of them fail? They failed for lack of Crystal Clarity. First, it was their intentions that were unclear. They didn't put spiritual principles first in their lives, but concentrated on outward, material goals: solar energy, new economic systems, revolutionary architectural concepts. Their idea of heaven on earth was of some system where everything material would function perfectly.

Given this approach to the ideal of finding a new life via the broad highway of matter, they were bound to fail.

One of the most persistent human delusions is the belief that good systems will produce good people. It is people, not systems, that need perfecting. Good systems will function well if the people running them have the good will to make them work. But if people have good will, even bad systems can be made to limp along somewhat successfully.

No mere economic system can possibly create a successful community. No mere decision to live and work together, without a Crystal Clear, high purpose in life, can possibly bond people in unity during stressful times. No merely social experiment will ever work.

What *will* work is people banding together to live for God, and in adherence to Godly principles. What will work is a life of sincere dedication—indeed, a new kind of monasticism, which includes families, schools, and businesses, but all of these normal activities directed lovingly in service of the highest possible ideal.

Religious communities, composed of families, and not only of single monastics, have been tried occasionally in the past. Some of them have worked successfully. None, however, have offered a viable prototype for modern times. For all of them defined their realities dogmatically, excluding from their sympathies all unbelievers. Their dogmatic approach to life forced their members into the service of abstract ideas. The ideas alone were the reality of those communities. Not even a subject for consideration was the contribution those ideas might make to the welfare of mankind.

Jesus had an answer for such dogmatism: "The Sabbath was made for man, and not man for the Sabbath."

No community can survive, except perhaps as an ideological fossil, if it cuts itself off from the greater society of which it is a part. Its very existence is justified, rather, by the service it renders to that society.

Always, and in all ways, communities must view themselves as part of a greater truth—a truth manifested on earth as well as in spirit. They must see themselves as part of the greater society; as part of the whole human race; as part of the great symphony of all life; above all, as part of the infinite reality that is God.

A body cannot survive without the head. The body of society, similarly, cannot survive without the guiding principles that flow downward from man's higher nature. Man must be guided by inspiration from above, or else find himself lost and struggling through a dark swamp of confusion. His confusion will begin on a spiritual level, but ere long it will descend to the mental level, and finally will bring about his destruction even on the physical level.

"All things forsake thee, who forsakest Me."

God, in modern times, has been all but forgotten by mankind. Is it any wonder that mankind wanders in darkness?

The time has come for people to live lives of even higher dedication than that which inspired monks and nuns in the past. Those dedicated souls lived lives that were focused on God, but theirs was also a spirit of negative denial of this world, which God made.

The time has come now for people to direct their spiritual awareness also *downward* into matter—to apply the principles of Crystal Clarity to everything they do: to their work, to education, to family life, to friendship, to their communications with strangers, to the way they build their homes—to all the most mundane, practical aspects of daily, human life.

Men need now to become God-centered *from within,* and from that center to see God everywhere, in everything.

Ananda's notable success as a community is owed principally to the observance of these principles. It is an experiment not only in community living, but in the creative *application* of the principles of Crystal Clarity to all aspects of human life.

Because it is only by the total application of these principles that the ideal of Cities of Light can come into existence, this book is not intended to woo its readers with tame, romantic dilutions that may sound attractive, but that will never work. My aim in these pages is to challenge you to reach up to the highest ideals of which you are capable; to challenge you to dedicate your life to that calling which alone can give you true life. The challenge is to embrace a new way of living, in many respects not an easy way, but one that is infinitely worth the effort.

For when I stand on the grounds of Ananda and look about me, I often think, as so many other members here have exclaimed, "If only people knew about all this. This is the *only* way they'd want to live!"

The Origins of Crystal Clarity

Chapter four

Crystal Clarity has only recently been defined as a guiding principle in itself. The identification, however, has been made on the basis of the teachings of a great mystic of modern times.

That mystic's name was Paramhansa Yogananda.

Yogananda's mission originated in India. What he taught, however, was not sectarian religion, but the Crystal Clarity of divine insight, which he radiated downward into the needs of modern man on every level.

He didn't separate spiritual realities from social or material or scientific realities. The high dedication to which he called people did not call for withdrawal into a cave or to a remote monastery. Rather, he sought to demonstrate divine solutions to the normal, human problems of everyday life.

In India, he founded a highly successful school. In this country, he created several successful businesses. He composed music, wrote poetry, was a keen sponsor of the arts.

He developed an organic farm, and taught the principles of right diet (which he called "Proper-eatarianism"!—to remove from it any implication of faddishness).

A few of his friends were prominent scientists. He even demonstrated his interest in a spiritual approach to the sciences by dedicating his *magnum opus,* the well-known spiritual classic, *Autobiography of a Yogi*, to Luther Burbank, the famous botanist, whom he termed "an American saint."

He was greatly interested in the advancement of human welfare through practical inventions (even suggesting a few of his own) and through social development of all kinds.

He was deeply interested in politics as they affected the well-being of society. Unlike those mystics who remove themselves from worldly realities, he was deeply concerned over certain of the directions that have been taken by modern society—for example, toward excessive centralization of government; toward inflation, which, speaking in the 1940s, he said would eventually destroy our economy; and toward social welfare programs, which he said enslaved the wills of the recipients.

Onto each of these mundane-seeming issues he brought to bear the Crystal Clarity of higher, spiritual vision, in order to show people that the time has come for mankind to integrate spirituality into the heart of its life, and not relegate it to an hour in church on Sundays, and to occasional readings from the Bible.

Yogananda brought to the West a new expression of truth—that aspect of spiritual teaching which is eternal. He needed to leave his own culture, that he might have the freedom to receive divine guidance without the restricting influence of old, cultural patterns of thought. His was a new wine; it needed new casks to fill, lest the old casks (to quote Jesus Christ) break.

The West, for its part, was in deep need of a new message—not one couched in old theological terminology and fixed dogmas, nor one delivered in a narrowly orthodox context, but one that was fresh, new, and open to the unique spiritual challenges of our times.

Here, too, the simile of the wine casks applies. What was needed was a new environment, not the old, long-used casks of established Christianity.

Probably only a person coming from outside our Western culture could have approached so vast a subject with so free a mind.

Yogananda found freedom in America to develop and expand his ideas. His stated purpose was not to convert people *from*, but rather *to,* true Christianity. His confrontation was with materialism, not with sincere devotion to God. Devotion he supported, no matter what form it took.

Jesus said, "Think not that I am come to destroy the law, and the prophets. I am not come to destroy, but to fulfill." Yogananda, similarly, came not to oppose the teachings of Christianity, but to show deeper truths in Christ's teachings, truths which people had forgotten. He came to show the deep relevance of Christ's teachings to human life on all levels. And he came, he said, to teach people how to meditate and commune inwardly with God.

His mission, as he often told people, was to bring back "the original Christianity of Jesus, and the original Hinduism of Krishna." In fact, it was to bring people back to the true essence of religion, which is not sectarian, but is intended to inspire soul-attunement with the Infinite Lord.

The eternal nature of truth Jesus himself expounded, when he said, "Before Abraham was, I am." The infinite nature of truth he expressed when he said, "Heaven and earth shall pass away, but my word shall not pass away."

Paramhansa Yogananda tried also to start a community for people who wanted to live together in God. During his lifetime, as it turned out, the time was not yet ripe for such an experiment.

He therefore empowered the work that has become Ananda World Brotherhood Village. He also placed his vibrations and his blessings "in the ether," as he put it, "in the spirit of God," that other communities in the future might flourish when the time was right. For he believed deeply in the need for an environment where people, whether married or single, might live together for God—a place where work, fellowship, and worship could be united in a harmonious whole.

Yogananda's constant emphasis was on principles, not on sectarian differences. Often he declared, "I did not come to America to found a sect." He wanted to inspire people to be guided not by blind beliefs, but, instead, by *tested* beliefs, and by what they found from their own experience really works.

One of the saddest developments in our age of materialistic cynicism is the revulsion that has been generated in the popular fancy against religious "cults" of all kinds. Suitable examples have been selected to create this wave of revulsion—groups that were wildly fanatical, or self-serving, or utterly lacking in charity to others, and even to their own.

That people have come, as a result of such publicized examples, to reject the efforts of sincere people to live Godly lives is worse than deplorable: It bodes disaster for the future of our civilization. For only by the uplifting force of a spiritual revival can society be saved from its present headlong plunge into spiritual confusion and total disbelief in any lasting verities. Without such a revival, the present direction of mankind must necessarily be toward the destruction of everything that mankind equates with progress.

What is a "cult"? It is a group of people whose system of beliefs prevents them from accepting any reality other than their own. It is a self-enclosed body of worshipers, separated from society at large by their beliefs, a group of people who either lose or renounce the ability to communicate with others, and who pit their own interests against those of others.

Such a body of people deservedly finds itself excluded by society, since it excluded society from its sympathies in the first place.

The charge of "cultishness," however, should not be limited to religious groups. *Any* social group for whom beliefs are more important than people, or than tested reality, commits the error of cultishness. Even individuals, if they reject others on the strength of ideational differences, are showing cultish attitudes by their rejection.

Mature people, even when they disagree, at least "agree to disagree." A person's ideas ought not to freeze out others from his sympathies. He should develop ideas, rather, as bridges to cross the chasm that forever separates man from man.

Yogananda was not a "cult leader." He was in every imaginable way the exact opposite. Where the people he met were often closed-minded, he himself kept his mind constantly open, and tried always to inspire them to do likewise. If people disagreed with him, he never tried to bend them to his point of view, but showed respect for their views, and even showed himself perfectly willing to change his own, should theirs prove right.

He was the perfect man of God for modern times. He displayed the Crystal Clarity of divine understanding as it relates to the problems and attitudes of our age. Yet he never descended from his own lofty vision, which was always rapt in God.

Such, then, was the inspiration and power that built Ananda.

Ananda has been the expression, on every level of its members' lives, of divine principles *in action*. Like the spokes of a wheel radiating outward from a hub, the various expressions of Crystal Clarity in the members' lives, in their work, and in their worship at Ananda are all creative applications of the central vision that Paramhansa Yogananda brought to the West, a vision which he himself sought to make relevant to the practical needs of mankind in this modern age.

Crystal Clarity in Business

Chapter five

Some years ago, Ananda bought East West Bookstore, in Menlo Park, California. Already famous at the time of purchase, it has since become one of the three or four leading metaphysical bookstores of its kind in America— probably, indeed, in the world.

The lady from whom the store was purchased had achieved her success through her unusually wide knowledge of the thousands of books in the store, and of their hundreds of authors. The Ananda members, however, who now had the job of running the shop, had only a very limited familiarity with the books and their authors. Following the approach to truth taken by Paramhansa Yogananda, they were more interested in direct spiritual experience than in reading about it vicariously in books. And yet, the bookstore seemed a worthwhile business for Ananda.

Crystal Clarity in salesmanship required an appraisal of why Ananda was there in the first place. Obviously, the goal was service. Even department stores, however, believe in serving people. Service in a consciousness of Crystal Clarity seemed to demand much more than satisfying the customers' desires.

As the central principles of Crystal Clarity were applied to salesmanship, new concepts began to emerge. One of Ananda's unofficial slogans is, "We communicate." In selling to people, it became clear that people need to be heard. They need answers in terms of their own realities, and not of the realities of those selling to them.

Very often, the customers' need to be heard wasn't related specifically to a request for any book, but to a need for deeper clarity in their lives. Better than any book, then, what an Ananda salesperson could try to do for them was tune in to them and try to hear what *their own higher self* was trying to say to them. For people often are too close to themselves to hear this inner guidance when it applies to them.

Crystal Clarity in dealing with the customers meant relating to them not as customers, but as divine friends—

even if they came with unfriendly attitudes. It meant trying to be an instrument of light, and to direct that light into all levels of their lives.

It meant mentally trying to bless them as they entered the store, and again as they left. It meant smiling at them from the heart, and with the eyes, not only with the lips.

It meant setting aside personal worries and annoyances, and asking God inwardly, "Help me to channel Your love to this person," or, "What would You like to give this person, through me, today?"

It meant looking beyond the personality of the customer, and relating to the Divine Presence within him.

Selling to people with this attitude is a wonderful spiritual practice. The Ananda salespeople began sitting regularly in meditation and silent inner communion before opening the doors to their customers for the day. They would pray that all who came into the shop would be blessed. They would pray that God use them as instruments of His peace and love.

Soon, people began visiting the store even if they had no books to buy. They came simply to greet the personnel, or to share some thought or discovery that they'd made that day. Members of many different spiritual paths found a sense of unity with one another in God's all-embracing love.

Ananda has bought, or created, many other businesses. All of them are successful, and for the same reasons of Crystal Clarity applied to situations where, normally, the sole motive would have been profit. What the principles of Crystal Clarity applied to profit revealed was that an enterprise is profitable not only if it earns money, but also if it repays those running it in terms of greater inner happiness, expanded sympathies, and a sense of usefulness and service to a higher cause. In each of the Ananda businesses, the same basic principles are conscientiously followed.

In an Ananda clinic, for example, the doctors and nurses begin each day with a prayer for their patients. While treating the patients as they come in, they try to channel God's healing energy to them, and not only to pass on medical information and advice.

Ananda businesses include a boutique, a restaurant and health food store, a woodworking shop, a home builders guild, a market, a publishing house, a recording studio, a car repair shop, shoemaking, artistic design, promotions, and many others. Some businesses are community owned; others are owned by individuals.

There is no problem with starting one's own business, provided it doesn't involve activity or products that are out of harmony with the basic principles of the community.

A number of members work outside the Ananda community structure, in nearby towns and cities. Some of them travel around the country in pursuance of their own professions, perhaps as lecturers, or writers, or in a number of other capacities.

All members and businesses pay a certain amount monthly to the community to help with Ananda's maintenance and development. Every effort is made by the community to work with those who, for a time, are not able to pay. Helpfulness to them includes assisting them to find work.

Crystal Clarity as applied to business means clarity in the normal business sense also. In this case, however, clarity assumes a spirit of freshness and creativity, and is not limited to the practical logic of bookkeeping.

The Creator of universes displays infinite creativity. New ways should be sought, similarly, to serve Him in this world with high, joyful, but realistically manifested energy. Graceful but meaningless gestures in the name of spirituality have little or no part to play in a truly spiritual life.

Yogananda used sometimes to speak wryly of the "romance of religion." By this expression he meant the outward trappings of religion, and those gestures and expressions which are so often associated with the religious life: the whispered "bless you"s, the saintly smiles, the pious sighs, the humbly downcast eyes, the fantastic irresponsibility. These, he would remark, are merely signs of beginners on the path. They soon wear off.

The truly spiritual person displays common sense and practicality, high energy, an attitude of constant even-mindedness and cheerfulness, and an effort always to relate to any reality with which life presents him.

The roots of spirituality, of course, are deep, inner devotion to God, a desire to please Him and to serve Him selflessly, and, at last, to be united with Him in His love. These deeper feelings, however, are not for outward show. Outwardly, they manifest themselves in kindness, friendly concern, compassion, and all the qualities that have made our businesses at Ananda the rendezvous for people from many walks of life—people who feel they are receiving something real, even if they don't always know exactly what it is.

Crystal Clarity in the Home

Chapter six

Most homes don't communicate. They are not what one might call *conscious* homes.

The majority are built with the purpose of shutting out the world. Their statement, such as it is, might be written over the front door in the words: "Our home is our castle. Don't intrude." Even homes that are built to impress others are, in their aura of wealth and standoffishness, an implicit statement of non-communication.

Frank Lloyd Wright tried to introduce a kind of communication into his homes. He conceived them as expressions of the natural environment in which they sat. The homes he built represent, however, an attempt to let the environment dictate the form of the building. Dictation is monologue; it is not communication.

The consciousness of the people living in Frank Lloyd Wright's homes wasn't really taken into consideration. His interiors were notoriously inconvenient. The owners were expected to adjust their lives to the impersonal demands of their environment, but not to interact with it.

In Cities of Light, the residents' homes should try to express consciously an interaction with their environment. And not only with their immediate, physical environment, but with their larger "environment" of immaterial realities—their ideas and ideals, the world of consciousness in which they live.

Creating a new environment, such as a City of Light, offers marvelous opportunities for rethinking one's life on every level. It is difficult, living in surroundings that are well established, to introduce new concepts into our lives. The hypnotic effect of mass consciousness, even when that consciousness is not clearly defined, is difficult to overcome.

The owners of a home in a certain housing tract, so I have heard, once put a gargoyle on the roof. So eccentric was the display considered that it became the talk of the community. Neighbors would drive out of their way to show it to their guests.

Imagine weighing anchor and sailing in new directions in the midst of such a psychic bog!

Here again we see the value of finding new casks for new wine: a new setting for the expression of new ideas.

The very term, Cities of Light, cries out for new architectural expressions. On the other hand, it defies any attempt at standardization. For light is not a form. It can be allowed entry by the shape forms take—by large windows, for example. It can be suggested by the way forms are shaped. No specific form, however, could ever define or limit the concept of light.

The concept of Crystal Clarity in home building should begin with the owners seeing their home as a conscious expression of their outlook on life. If they have made the choice to live in Crystal Clarity, then it follows that everything they do should represent a reaching out toward greater realities. That reaching out should express itself in their homes as well.

Homes should be built not to shut out reality, but to permit communication with reality on one's own terms. They could never seem homelike if they didn't grant the owners privacy as well. Homes should be restful. They can, however, state their own reality without rejecting all other realities. If the owners are secure enough in themselves, their conscious self-expression in the form and style of their home can afford to be more relaxed, and not try with stern rigidity to exclude the world, as houses generally do.

Home building should begin from the inside—from the owners' philosophy of life, from how they view their environment, and from how they see the world. If they love people, they ought to show that love by creating a home with beautiful lines, so that it enhances what other people see of the environment, instead of merely obstructing their view of it. If they love their environment, they may want large, high windows that permit participation in their surroundings. If they have high ideals, they may want their homes in some way to express a soaring consciousness, and not build them to sit squatly on the landscape as though hoping never again to be budged.

One's home should *suggest* a larger reality than that which it actually expresses. Homes built in a City of Light ought to represent a conscious reaching out to reality *as light*. To accomplish this end, they could create a sense of inner space, of expanding awareness. They could open outward to some part of the surrounding world, instead of closing inward upon themselves.

Long, low ceilings, ending at the far end of the room in low windows, give somewhat the impression that one is wearing a visor. If, for economic reasons, the ceilings have to be built low, perhaps at least a portion of some room might be built to rise upward, expansively. The extra cost of higher ceilings, however, may not be as great as one thinks, and may well be worth the trouble anyway. One's home, after all, is something one expects to enjoy for many years — long after the initial costs have been forgotten.

A person's home should in some way reflect his own attitudes toward life. It should, however, reflect only those aspects of his attitudes which uplift his consciousness. It should help him to affirm that part of his nature which he wants to encourage, and not be a constant reminder of negative attitudes which, though perhaps true to some of his present realities, he would like to overcome in himself. In this way, too, his home should be a *conscious* home.

He might try, when building his home, to suggest through its design his philosophy of life. The home ought at the same time to be a flexible, not a dogmatic, statement. For if he is trying to live in Crystal Clarity, his understanding is sure to develop and expand over the years. He would be wise, therefore, to construct his home in such a way as to give him latitude for development within himself towards ever-greater maturity. The home he constructs should give his consciousness the freedom to expand.

Much more can be expressed through the lines of a building than most people realize. It is fascinating to see how a simple line may, perhaps quite inexplicably, express some feeling, or some state of mind.

An upward curve may express a mood of joy. Wavy lines may express uncertainty. Too many sharp angles may express lack of flexibility. Curved lines, on the other hand, may express adaptability, and also inner harmony. A downward-curving line may express pessimism, or disappointment.

Lines that close inward upon a window seem to want to exclude the world. Lines, by contrast, that move outward, or upward, toward the view seem to want to reach out and embrace it.

A high entrance to the home calls to the neighbors, "Welcome." A low entrance says to them, "Enter only if you must."

Even when one buys a home instead of building it, there is much that he can do to adapt the home to his consciousness and philosophy of life.

Colors, for example, are vitally important as expressions of states of mind. Whatever the shape of a house, its colors can be changed at any time.

Light colors express expanding awareness. Dark colors, especially if they are dull, absorb energy; they have a dimming effect on one's awareness.

Even the shape of small sections of the building can be altered, at a relatively low cost. It is often surprising how a little alteration, well thought out in advance, can affect the whole feeling of a much larger structure.

Furniture is an obvious way of expressing personality, and even beliefs.

Because I myself believe deeply in world brotherhood, I've bought for my own home over the years a wide selection of furniture, paintings, and other objects from various parts of the world. Because all these items are things I loved when I saw them, a thread of unity runs through them — a community, one might almost say, of friendly feeling.

The pictures that people select for their homes are usually chosen without much thought for the fact that, every time a painting is hung on a wall, the artist's vibrations are being invited into the home. The better the artist, the more important it is for you to make sure you like his vibrations, for a good artist will more clearly express his consciousness and vibrations through his art. If what he depicts doesn't harmonize with your real feelings about life, why invite him into your home as an unpaying—indeed, well paid!— permanent guest?

The pictures a person hangs in his home should be thought of as members of the family—loved, cherished, and enjoyed anew every time he looks at them.

Enjoyment, and even fun, might also be considered when building a home. In my home at Ananda, for instance— because the only thing I miss here is the sea—I lined the walls of the stairwell to the basement with a large photo mural of the ocean. To add to the fun, I attached a little cassette tape recorder, with an external speaker, to the electric light switch. The recorder holds a tape recording of the ocean surf. How delightedly people laugh when I turn on the light and lead them downstairs into that ocean scene!

Downstairs in a corner, I even created a little area with sand from the island of Kauai, and an assortment of sea shells.

A home that is built according to the principles of Crystal Clarity should itself, on every level possible, be a channel of clarity.

All this is possible to do in an environment where one's whole life, and the lives of all one's friends, are lived in a spirit of consciously reaching out in attunement with high principles. In Cities of Light, it is possible to live creatively on every level of one's existence.

Such creativity in a person's life never becomes dull or boring, and never does it become exhausting. For that which exhausts people is the weight of matter-consciousness; never the freedom of expanding awareness, and the consciousness of light.

Crystal Clarity in Relationships

Chapter seven

In human relationships, it is surprising to see how seldom people really try to communicate. They may talk *at* one another. Or, if they listen at all, they may talk *to* one another—as if to say, "I've heard what you have to say, and this is my answer." But how few take the trouble to talk *with* people—to communicate with them openly, appreciatively, and sincerely.

The problem is a part of the general human predicament: People seem almost to *try* not to live consciously. They go through life like travelers in a subway, staring blankly at the floor until the journey's end. Admittedly, however, if no one around you wants to communicate, it is natural to find yourself willy-nilly engaging in monologue.

Cities of Light offer the marvelous opportunity of a life surrounded by people with whom one can share, and not merely coexist.

A few months ago I was eating in a restaurant with a few friends from Ananda. I suddenly realized that I'd been straining to listen to the conversation at the table next to ours. That isn't the sort of thing I normally do. Surprised, I took stock of myself and realized that it wasn't so much the topic of the conversation that attracted me. In fact, I hadn't really been following it. What had intrigued me was the simple fact that the people were talking about things that didn't involve them, personally.

One doesn't often hear that kind of conversation. At Ananda, one becomes accustomed to discussions covering a broad range of creative, impersonal ideas. Elsewhere, one often finds people so absorbed in themselves that their conversation seldom touches on anything that doesn't affect their lives personally.

Conversations are a delight when they can soar, explore, and expand one's consciousness. They do so naturally, when people come together in a sharing not only of interests, but ideals. Conversation becomes even more enjoyable when the ideals those people share include an aspiration to live in Crystal Clarity.

In one's association with other people, Crystal Clarity means *seeking always to include their realities in one's own.*

By including their realities, we can expand our own awareness, our own perception of reality.

It isn't easy to listen, when there doesn't seem to be anything to listen to. Normal, worldly conversation is rather like "white sound"; its function seems to be to reduce the impact of thought, rather than to stimulate thinking. One develops a habit, in the midst of vapid chatter, of listening with only a fraction of the mind. One needs the stimulation of intelligent, searching minds, of people with open, responsive feelings. In such an environment, disagreement ceases to be a confrontation, and becomes instead a mutual endeavor to arrive at clearer perceptions of reality.

In such an environment especially, people help one another to grow—mentally, emotionally, and, above all, spiritually. A community whose members are sincerely committed to developing their own understanding is not a confrontational community. Confrontation occurs when people want merely to affirm their own realities, not to expand them to include the realities of others, nor to reach outward in company with them to embrace wider realities. Confrontation never happens when people seek to develop themselves inwardly, and to encourage such development in others. With such a basic attitude, the natural tendency, whenever difficulties arise in one's relations with others, is to see self-correction as the obvious point of departure. Criticism of others thus becomes reduced to a minimum.

Indeed, one of the automatic insights derived from a consciousness of Crystal Clarity is that the wish to criticize springs from some kindred flaw in one's own character. Criticism, then, becomes self-exposure—a development not always intended! It is better to check the impulse to criticize against an impartial view of one's own inner feelings, to see whether the impulse arises from charitable sentiments, or from darker motives of judgment.

Normally, in any case, it is better not to offer criticism unless it is asked for, and even then not unless one feels intuitively that it is *right* to make a suggestion. For the wrong words spoken at the wrong time have often destroyed precious friendships.

Communities of people who sincerely want to improve themselves, and to encourage others with similar aspirations, are excellent laboratories of human behavior. Even negative examples, in such a setting, can often point to positive lessons.

I cited one such example earlier: the members of Ananda—during its early days, mostly—who lived primarily for themselves, and the contrast they made with others who lived with the interests of everyone at heart. In community life, the whole spectrum of selfish vs. unselfish behavior tends to become exposed for what it is, usually more clearly than in a society where people haven't self-improvement in mind. One sees examples numerous enough to be convinced that what one is observing reveals principles of human behavior, and not merely the peculiarities of individuals.

In Ananda's early days, especially, there was little understanding among many of the new members of the principle of genuine sharing, simply because they had come with little experience of it so far in their lives. Some of them felt fully justified in thrusting their own desires at everyone, in pursuing their private needs first, and in insisting that they first needed to seek their own security.

Others took the opposite course. They listened respectfully to others' needs, made the general welfare of everyone their priority, and saw the security of the entire community as their best guarantee of personal security as well.

What soon became obvious was that those who drifted toward the first end of the spectrum were never happy. Instead, they found more and more cause to complain at everything. It seemed, moreover, that they never managed to fulfill even their simplest desires. It was as though every goal receded before their reach. No matter how they struggled, they never attained the security they craved.

Such people either changed, usually under the inspiration of others' beneficial examples, or they left.

The other group of members, however, were always happy. Moreover, they seemed in unaccountable ways to have everything they ever wanted or needed. Security was never a problem for them, both because they didn't seek it and because it sought them, unasked. The more Ananda prospered, the more they automatically prospered, too. And during those times when Ananda went through hard times financially, their efforts, added to the cooperative efforts of many, raised the whole community back to a level of prosperity.

Gradually, everyone in the community came to understand, and on ever-deeper levels of reality, the *sheer personal fulfillment* that comes from living in cooperation and harmony with others.

They came to see their relationships, finally, as channels for the expression of that Larger Reality with which they were seeking to attune their lives.

Relationships in a community that is dedicated to the ideal of living for God, and in God, are divine friendships in which each member seeks communion with God not only in his meditations, but also through his friends. He loses the worldly habit of "hobnobbing" with others in mutually belittling familiarity. Rather, having felt God's presence in the silence within, he sees all things, and all people everywhere, as opportunities for communing with that Presence without.

Relationships in such a community are based on mutual, divine respect. And this is one important reason, certainly, why community life, rightly developed, is so remarkably free of friction.

Once, moreover, people come together not only for diversion, nor to escape reality, but with love above all for truth, they voluntarily subordinate their personal opinions to the search for truth in every situation.

With mutual, divine respect for one another; sincere dedication to *what is* (as opposed to what might be); a conditioned tendency, in any disagreement, to examine their own motives first; a commitment to the welfare of everyone; and, above all, with sincere love for God, it really is not difficult for a community of people to live in joyful harmony together.

Lest all these conditions seem difficult to meet, remember that a mountain is climbed one step at a time. An axiom of biology is, "Nature never makes sudden leaps." This statement is certainly true regarding human nature. When one realizes that self-transformation requires time, he develops a more tolerant attitude toward himself as well as towards others. He takes his daily step at a time. One day, all in a flash, he realizes that the job really hasn't been so difficult after all!

The mountain looks less imposing when you're half-way up it.

One of the benefits of living in a City of Light is the impact one's life has on the broader community of society at large.

Suppose a thousand people, dedicated to these ideals, were to live and work in a thousand different cities. Assuming all were able to remain true to their ideals—a bold assumption in itself!—how far-reaching would the example of each be of a life lived in Crystal Clarity, and of harmonious, joyful living?

These people might find themselves generally admired (an admiration which in itself might prove more a temptation than a reward, causing them to think highly of themselves, and thereby to lose touch with their ideals). They might even find themselves envied. With all this admiration and envy, however, it is more than likely that others would never see them as anything but unique, and as fortunate in the possession of such radiant personalities. No one at all, possibly, would draw from their example the inspiration to change himself.

It is when many people live together, and begin to display attractive attitudes, and magnetism in their smiles, that others begin to see that what are involved here are universal principles of human nature, and not a few unusual personalities.

It is the same as with the lessons learned from the variety of behavior within the community itself: Numerous examples, all of them together in one place, and viewed together in a continuous time sequence, can offer a lesson with an impact that is unforgettable.

Most of the virtues acquired on the spiritual path come not with specific, heroic effort applied to developing the virtues themselves. They are the natural companions, rather, of a gradual expansion of a person's awareness and sympathies. It is not difficult to forgive others, when you feel kindly disposed toward everyone. And it is not difficult to feel kindly disposed, when you no longer feel that your own realities have forever to be protected against a potentially hostile world.

It is not difficult to accept trying situations, moreover, if your heart is fixed on eternity. In such a view, longer rhythms become your reality, and the inconveniences of the moment are inevitably seen as but ripples on a much larger wave.

It is not difficult to adjust your desires to those of others, if your attachment is to greater realities.

And it is not difficult, finally, to view everything with good humor, if, within yourself, you know happiness.

Crystal Clarity in Leadership

Chapter eight

Essential to the concept of living in Crystal Clarity in a community is the relation of this concept to the question of leadership. For as the body requires a head; as a community, by the same token, requires high ideals to hold it together; so also do group activities require leadership.

With leadership of the wrong kind, even the most worthwhile undertakings can become diverted into wrong avenues. Without leadership of any kind, however, even the best of projects rarely gets beyond the front gate.

Leadership, more than any other aspect of life in a City of Light, needs to hold Crystal Clarity as its central reality.

First, and most important, leadership in a City of Light should be inclusive. It should not be a one-man show. Least of all can it succeed if it is dictatorial. Crystal Clarity as applied to leadership may perhaps be best defined as *supportive leadership*.

Cities of Light are bound to succeed, in time, for the realities of this age demand them. They will succeed, however, only when those who hold positions of leadership within them see their role in terms, not of glory, but of responsibility; when they understand that the important thing is what they *give* to the job, not what they receive back from it.

Let us see what this sort of leadership entails. And let me remind the reader, lest he wonder whether such leadership is really possible, that a sincere commitment to truth gives rise naturally to generous attitudes. There is nothing particularly heroic about them.

Most people's image of leadership has been molded by stories of executives whose consuming desire was to "get ahead," or of square-jawed generals in the smoke of battle, gazing far-seeingly into the distance. With such images in mind, it is natural that the promise of supportive leadership should compare somewhat less than favorably with the proverbial "impossible dream." Supportive leadership, however, turns out on close inspection to be nothing, really, but the expression of an expanded view of reality.

A crystal is notable for its capacity to transmit light instead of blocking it. The clearer the crystal, the greater also its beauty; but its beauty is owed to the simple fact that, being clear, it transmits light.

Crystal Clarity in leadership, then, means the consciousness of being the instrument, rather than the origin, of inspiration. It means recognizing that inspiration is not a personal property, and may come equally to anyone; that it should be taken, therefore, on merit regardless of its source.

Crystal Clarity in leadership means commitment to truth, not to opinion—just as in every other aspect of community life and relationships.

A leader's concern should be with getting things done, not with what people might think of him in the process. He should, however, weigh their opinions of him impartially as part of his commitment to truth, and change himself, or his directions, if he sees that his critics are right.

The feelings of others, moreover, must be seen as part of the reality with which he has to deal, so that even if he knows they are mistaken, he must sometimes give preference to their right to err over what might be the still greater error of imposing his will on them.

Leadership means rendering service, not receiving it. It means giving loyalty first to others, and perhaps not even demanding it of them in return.

Crystal Clarity in leadership means working with people as they *are,* not as the leader might like them to be. It requires great patience to work with people. Sometimes it may even be obvious to everyone that a certain person needs to change himself in some respect. Yet, if he is not ready to receive the correction, what is the point of raising the issue? A leader must develop the habit of speaking to useful purpose.

People's readiness to be corrected needs always to be considered. Indeed, this is not only a question of the leader's need for patience, but of his sheer need to be practical. For good advice offered at the wrong moment may, by the rejecting energy that it engenders in the recipient, and by its remembered wave of resistance, make it all the more difficult for the recipient to accept the same advice in the future, when perhaps the moment *is* right.

One difficulty for anyone in a position of responsibility is that the final decision is always his. Others may theorize with wild abandon, pleading their cause with desperate sincerity. They can afford to do so. Theirs isn't the burden of final commitment to a definite line of action.

It is like money: If a project doesn't entail spending your money, you may enthusiastically urge the commitment of millions to it. Should you realize, however, that the work will have to be financed entirely out of your own pocket, how many dollars will you commit? Hundreds? Or, possibly, none at all? You may discover, at any rate, a fresh need to study all the details and make sure the project is both practical and really desirable.

A leader, in other words, must be one who can accept the burden not only of criticism (he is bound to attract some of that anyway), but of *meriting* the criticism. He must be able to admit it when he has erred, and have the inner strength not to crumble under the weight of his self-recognition. Thus, he must not only be dedicated to truth, but have a sufficiently broad base of self-acceptance for the gusts of controversy not to shatter his equilibrium.

He must be a person of intuition, but that intuition must be held firmly in rein by common sense.

The supportive leader must of course also be flexible. For no matter how desirable a direction, his more important job is not finding good directions, merely, but getting everyone behind those directions.

In leadership, more than in any other aspect of life in Cities of Light, the golden principle of community life must always be kept in mind: *People are more important than things*.

One weakness of human nature is people's tendency, during deliberations, to see talk as a substitute for action. Crystal Clarity in leadership means also, then, realizing that it is action that generates creative energy, much more so than talk.

It may sometimes be better to follow a less-than-ideal course of action than to let deliberations bog down in endless debate. For there comes a point in every deliberation when further discussion can only drain a project of energy. When this point is reached, even an imperfect decision may sometimes prove better in the long run than continued indecision. At least it keeps open the channels of creativity.

Crystal Clarity in leadership means, finally, understanding that the quality of product depends on the kind of energy that went into producing it. If you want harmonious results from any project undertaken by a group, you must proceed throughout with harmony. If once the harmony is lost, it may be better to abandon the project altogether.

I remember one occasion, years ago, when Ananda was in the process of purchasing a store for one of its businesses. The location was desirable. The store itself was desirable. As the conclusion of negotiations was being approached, however, the store owner became unreasonably angry over some trifle. Perhaps this was simply his way of bargaining. At any rate, Ananda immediately stopped all further negotiations. The general feeling among the members involved was that if the deal couldn't be conducted in harmony, it was better not to conclude it at all.

In fact, the less attractive-seeming alternative which this cancellation of negotiations forced upon the community proved in the end to be a much better deal, overall.

Supportive leadership means cooperation. Its constant aim, therefore, is to solicit cooperation, not unthinking obedience, from others. People must be inspired as much as possible to feel that the leadership is actually coming from them—as, in fact, ideally it generally should be.

Leadership of this type, when possible, is not a strain on anyone, but a mutually joyful interaction. Such leadership, however, will only work as a joint effort. The leader who tries to get others to lead before they are ready to participate will find himself dealing with countless warring factions.

I've devoted much space to leadership as a downward flow from above, like the relationship between the head and the body. The fact of human dynamics is that group ventures rarely, if ever, get off the ground without the inspiration, and the focused dedication, of one person. As Emerson put it, "An institution is the lengthened shadow of one man." Creativity comes from inside. It can't very well result from a procedure that puts everything to a vote.

The better established a direction, however, the more it needs to become a community direction, and to be subject to community decisions. Thus, leadership should strive ever more fully to involve others in the process of leadership.

Fortunately, given any difficulty a leader might experience in sharing his role, the very circumstances attending an organization's growth make his job an increasing burden to him, unless he has the inner freedom to agree to share his leadership with others. For with growth comes complexity, and with complexity the necessity for making endless decisions that are not even creative, but merely time-consuming.

Thus, Nature herself creates the circumstances whereby a leader with clear inner guidance cannot but realize the fitness of turning over the reins to others. One of his principal jobs as a leader, then, is always to be on the lookout for people who can truly lead others, and not merely drive them.

The kind of community described in this book—a City of Light—is, in a sense, a monastery, even if its members are married. For Cities of Light offer a way of life for those who want to live wholly for God. Anything less than sincere dedication, as I have said already, will not work, and will become diluted in no time to resemble the countless towns and cities in America where economic considerations and self-interest reign supreme in every decision that is made.

Guidance from above, not from below, is the essence of the monastic way of life, for which I have used the metaphor of the head and the body. A monastery, to function as such, must have a spiritual head, chosen for his wisdom, and not for his ability to please a sufficient number of political factions.

Ideally—and this is the solution that has been found at Ananda—a community needs, on the one hand, a spiritual director and a spiritual directorate; and on the other hand, a general manager, or group of managers, elected by the community, to manage the more outward aspects of community life.

The concern of the spiritual directorate should be not only the spiritual life of the community, but the rightness, spiritually speaking, of any major decision.

Here is an example of the interaction being described here between the spiritual directorate and the managing body.

One time, the managing group at Ananda wanted to deny a member certain demands of his which they considered unreasonable.

The spiritual director addressed the issue in something like the following words: "Reasonableness and unreasonableness are not always the issue when working with people. Their capacity to be reasonable isn't always reliable. It seems to me that what we must do here is practice compassion."

"But it's a matter of principle," argued a spokesman for the managerial side.

"If you were ill," replied the spiritual director, "wouldn't you want to feel you had the community's support? This person is ill. It's just that his illness isn't physical, since it affects his mental clarity. Isn't compassion, then, a higher principle? If this were really a matter of setting a precedent, the case would be different. But this case stands pretty much alone."

Thus, the demands were accepted, though with debatable results. For the member left the community—a direction in which he was headed anyway. But at least the community leadership affirmed, and clarified in the process, the importance of basing every decision in a City of Light on spiritual values.

Representatives in the governing body of Ananda are elected to represent different areas in the far-flung community. To help preserve a spirit of unity throughout the community, three more representatives are elected to represent the community at large. The duty of these three "representatives at large" is to help maintain a unified view of Ananda's needs.

Members are always welcome to attend the council meetings, and to voice their opinions. Matters involving a major shift of direction for the community, moreover, always have been put to a community vote.

There is an interesting problem, one that is often encountered among groups where the tide of new members is continuous. It arises from the fact that new people tend to be more easily impressed by the talkers in the community than by the doers. To make matters worse, those who prefer talking to acting tend, in any community, to seek out whomever they can impress with their talk. Older members, who know them well, may long since have given up on their empty eloquence. To whom, then, will they gravitate? Obviously, they will seek out the newcomers.

The danger is that such people may be voted into positions for which they are simply not qualified, where the influence they exert may prove disruptive. The simplest solution to this problem, and the one in operation at Ananda, is not to give people the right to vote until they've been members of the community for one year. A year, it is felt, is long enough for them to reach an understanding, based on their own experience, of the true state of affairs.

There is another potential danger in a community's development, especially if its development is as rapid as it has been at Ananda. The possibility exists that the old-timers might someday find themselves out-voted by a majority of newcomers who want the community to move in a direction different from the community's longstanding self-definition, and inconsistent with its inherent philosophy.

Ananda's solution to this potential problem—which, I might add, so far has not arisen—has been for the land itself to be placed under the control of members who have been here for five or more years. These long-term members correspond to those monks or nuns in a monastery who have taken their final vows. In fact, final vows are involved also in this case.

The turnover at Ananda through the years has been remarkably small. The present number of members who have taken final vows, therefore, dedicating their lives unreservedly to God, is large.

An important point for promoting harmony in the group dynamics of a community has proved to be the insistence that people need to demonstrate the right to be heard. People who set themselves up as "negative voices," in other words, should be asked to suggest positive solutions. Alternatively, they might be appointed, if possible, to correct the situations they have criticized.

By taking this positive approach to negativity, the whole community is soon brought around to positive attitudes. In fact, this problem, which existed in the early years at Ananda, is hardly ever encountered now.

There is truth in everyone, for everyone is a temple of God, though not always, as yet, conscious of the fact. If well-meaning people are involved in an undertaking, and if they work together sensitively, with a combination of wisdom and love, there is no reason why the old belief in people's inability to live and work together harmoniously need continue to hold true. Monks and nuns have managed to live harmoniously in communities for centuries.

What is needed today is to expand the definition of monasticism, so that the only alternative to its traditionally rigid rule need not forever be a steep descent into egotism and worldliness.

Crystal Clarity in Marriage

Chapter nine

A sad aspect of marriage in modern times, and particularly of marriage in America, is the high incidence of divorce. It betokens a breakdown of fundamental values—of commitment, for example, to the feelings and well-being of others; of loyalty to others, and to an ideal; of the recognition that difficulty in the fulfillment of one's duty never constitutes a valid reason for abandoning that duty; of the understanding that to live rightly is a long-range proposition, and should not be influenced by short-term "solutions" that offer merely a way out.

On the other hand, there is also a positive aspect to the divorce rate. For it isn't likely that people's reasons for getting married have changed all that radically in this century. Even though, nowadays, too many marriages fail, this doesn't mean that in olden times all marriages were "made in heaven."

The truth is, many marriages in times past, when divorce was virtually unheard of, were things not of beauty, but of great suffering and bitterness for both partners. It is far better, surely, for people to separate who otherwise would be forced to live together in constant, mutual disharmony and friction.

The solution, then, is not to approach the problem symptomatically, by studying the causes for divorce and how to minimize them. Rather, it is to study the reasons for marriage, to see how valid they are, and how to get people to enter into marriage with greater clarity and self-understanding.

Cities of Light offer people of good will an opportunity to develop new ways of looking at everything, and in the process to find new ways of solving old problems.

Solutions to the major problems in human life usually require the cooperative interaction of many people. If those people speak from many different premises, however, communication becomes almost as difficult as in a roomful of people talking different languages. Discouragement and fatigue eventually cause a breakdown of further communication, and the problems end up looking more insoluble than ever.

Every great movement in history, whether in art, science, religion, or any other field, was born out of groups of people who shared basically the same interests and premises, and who found themselves in a position to communicate creatively with one another. One might almost say that their combined energy produced the magnetism that attracted the inspiration, which seemed to settle on them for the duration of that energy-flow.

The fact of those movements is well established. This explanation for them, however, is my own, and ought perhaps to be further elaborated.

Could Beethoven, for instance, have written the music he did had it not been for the other composers of his era: Bach, Haydn, Mozart, and the rest? The question might be moot were it not for the fact that history shows us so very few examples of isolated greatness.

Here, then, we see one of the supreme benefits that may, and in fact should, reflect back to society as a whole from the creation of Cities of Light. A group of people interacting creatively with one another, and not merely shouting one another down, ought surely to discover, and bring to outward manifestation, new solutions to countless old problems.

Some of these opportunities for new discovery we have touched on already. Another such opportunity, and a vital challenge to our entire society, is the institution of marriage.

Not only is a bad marriage a tragedy because of the pain it causes the two people involved, but also for the much deeper scars it inflicts on the children, if any, of their marriage. It is no cure, however, merely to stop people short of taking the final step of divorce. The tragedy was written already in the marriage itself.

Part of the answer, surely, lies in sorting out the couple's emotional, mental, and spiritual "chemistry" at the time when they first show an interest in each other. It is important that someone, or a group of people, help them to see whether they are truly compatible.

People need better reasons than the movies give them for getting married in the first place. Many, indeed, would have done better to confine their relationship to a friendly wave from opposite ends of an aisle at the supermarket.

The whole idea of marriage for reasons as ephemeral as sexual attraction has generally proved to be a disaster. Any children, moreover, born to couples that are forever torn between passion and disharmony are likely only to fan the flames of their disharmony.

The meaning of marriage needs to be explored in depth. The chemistry of attraction between two people needs to be better understood. The very education of young people in the realities of sex needs to take place in a higher context—from above, so to speak: from a level of high ideals, even of divine love, rather than from below, with the emphasis placed wholly on the animal aspects of procreation.

The very ceremony of marriage needs to be made a statement of lofty commitment on the couple's part—a commitment not only to each other, but to truth, and to God. Marriages that involve little more than the signing of a legal contract in a county courthouse are a travesty. Small wonder that so many people today speak of marriage as though all it meant was "a silly piece of paper."

Marriage, however, made sincerely before God, and in full understanding of what the commitment means, must surely have much greater chances of success than a quickie ceremony performed before fidgeting witnesses before a justice of the peace.

It is an interesting fact that, even in communist countries—or perhaps I should say, in Rumania, which is the one communist country I have visited—the preference of the party faithful is to have their weddings performed in church. Even atheists, then, so it would seem, sense the importance of adding to marriage some nobler commitment, some solemn ceremony that will endow the occasion with an importance beyond the mere signing of legal forms.

People nowadays are often heard to ask, "Why should one get married? If two people love each other, why shouldn't they simply live together? What difference does a piece of paper make?"

The simple answer is that, when a marriage is sincerely entered into before God, with a ceremony performed in a spirit of blessing by a priest or a minister, there is a grace that can be felt almost tangibly in the air. This sense of blessing can carry a couple through many crises in the years to come, crises which, in less spiritually based marriages, would cause an irreparable rift.

A meaningful wedding ceremony is certainly an important ingredient in a successful marriage. Apart from the blessing it invokes, two people who aren't compatible in the highest sense may think twice before getting married, if beforehand they are faced with a lofty statement of what marriage really means.

Cities of Light offer an ideal opportunity for the study of this problem. It is a challenge that faces Ananda also, where people have had to deal with previously conditioned attitudes and expectations. The problem is being seriously addressed by the entire community, and, bit by bit, solutions are being found. There is reason to hope that radical new insights will provide a basis for truly happy and mutually supportive marriages.

An important step has been taken at Ananda with the creation of a wedding ceremony that invites the couple to approach their marriage in full awareness that they are participating in a reality much greater than their own.

Much of the difficulty in marriages is the tendency to focus on problems of the moment, and on energies that are being generated at a minuscule point on the vast stage of life. When a couple can keep in mind life's longer rhythms, and the greater context for every present reality, they also find it easier to hang on to the central reality of their marriage, which is, simply, their love and commitment to each other.

It may be helpful at this point to include excerpts from the Ananda wedding ceremony, partly so that the reader may have a clearer idea of what it means to be married "in God," and partly to show what I mean by a monastic commitment in the context of marriage and family.

ANANDA WEDDING CEREMONY

(EXCERPTS)

(After a brief period of prayer and meditation, the bride and bridegroom offer roses to each other and say:)

> Dear beloved, I offer you this rose
>
> As a symbol of my love for you;
>
> A love inspired by God,
>
> And offered to you as a channel of His love.

SONG: *(These words may also be spoken, rather than sung, by the priest or minister.)*

> Where He dwells, the earth in gladness
>
> Puts forth sweet herbs, shading trees.
>
> Gay streams bound through summer meadows;
>
> Fragrance blows on every breeze.

They with happiness are blessed

Who the Lord have made their Guest—

Who the Lord have made their Guest.

Priest or minister:

In all things, see the hand of God;

And seek, through them, His blessing on your union.

From rocks and earth, seek steadfastness in love;

(He places a touch of earth on the forehead of each, at a point between the eyebrows.)

From water and all liquid things: the grace to flow through life in harmony, without attachment, in a spirit of acceptance and cooperation;

(He sprinkles a little water on their heads.)

From air and sweet fragrances: pure freedom from all thought of "I" and "mine";

(He holds steadily before them a few sticks of burning incense.)

And from rising fire, the understanding that human love must ever aspire toward the heights of perfect, divine love.

(He lights a fire in a metal bowl. Once the flames begin to rise, he says:)

In fire we see also a symbol of the unifying power of God's love, uniting your separate flames of life in His one, infinite light. Offer yourselves mentally into the fire of that love.

Repeat after me:

O Infinite love,

I offer myself up to Thee.

Burn up and purify my limitations.

(Bride and groom each offer a stick of wood into the flames.)

Destroy in me the seeds of earthly desire.

(They each cast a handful of rice into the fire.)

Accept my pure aspiration to be one with Thee.

(They pour a little clarified butter into the flames.)

HOLY VOWS AT MARRIAGE

(Expressed first by the couple to God:)

Beloved Lord,

We dedicate to Thee our lives, our service, and the love we share.

May the communion we find with one another lead us to inner communion with Thee.

May the service we render one another perfect in us our service of Thee.

May we behold Thee always enshrined in one another's forms.

May we always remember that it is above all Thee we love.

In every test of love, may we see Thy loving hand.

In any disagreement, may we see Thy hidden guidance.

May our love not be confined by selfish needs,

But give us strength ever to expand our hearts

Until we see all human beings, all creatures as our own.

Teach us to love all beings equally, in Thee.

(The couple then speak these vows to each other:)

Dear Beloved,

I will be true to you as I pray always to be true to God.

I will love you without condition, as I would be loved
by you

And as we are ever loved by God.

I will never compete with you; I will cooperate always
for our own, and for all others', highest good.

I will forgive you always, and under all circumstances.

I will respect your right to see truth as you perceive it,

And to be guided as you feel deeply within yourself,

And I will work with you always, in freedom, to arrive
at a common understanding.

All that we do, may we do for God's glory.

May we live and grow together in His love and joy.

And may the offspring of our union

Whether human children, or creative deeds

Be doorways for the inspiration that we feel from Him,

Through each other.

May our love grow ever deeper, purer, more expansive,

Until, in our perfected love,

We find the perfect love of God.

Crystal Clarity in Education

Chapter ten

The predicament of marriage in modern society underscores an even greater problem: the education that we give our young. We teach children how to solve problems in mathematics, but give them nothing to help them solve the problems in their personal lives. We flood them with a tide of factual information, then tell them, as we send them out the door with their diplomas, "It's up to you now to figure out what it all means."

The problem itself is overwhelming. We live in an age of constant new discoveries, many of them staggeringly important to our understanding of life and of the universe around us. Astronomers seem constantly to be finding out new things about the universe that invalidate one or another of the basic assumptions of physics. Darwin's theory of evolution, itself a cornerstone of modern man's understanding of life, has been coming under fire from leading scientists.

Who can guess what will come next? Only the other day a physicist, Paul Cottle, succeeded in adding three protons to an atom of gold, thereby converting it into lead.

The vast number of new facts themselves are difficult to gather and sift, so that students can receive them in some semblance of order. How, then, can teachers be expected to make time for the study of human values? The very importance of re-plowing all that old land, when so much new territory beckons to be explored, must seem to many of them the sort of reminder that gets filed away in offices "for future consideration." Moral values, nowadays, seem as though they lacked the stirring immediacy of scientific research.

When one is running at full speed down a long flight of stairs, how easy is it for him to stop, even if you call to tell him that his shoelaces are untied? Still, if for a moment he can catch his thoughts along with his breath, it may dawn on him that those dangling shoelaces might easily cause him to stumble, and that if he should do so he might get seriously hurt.

It may be difficult for our harried educators, as well, to pause a moment and think what they're really accomplishing in their jobs. They've built up so much momentum in the process of gathering all that information, and of shoveling it onward to their students in the classrooms.

Someone, however, needs to think through the deeper implications of what the children are being taught. If teachers can't take the time to do so—and it seems that problems are seldom solved by the people most involved in them—then others must be found who are freer to take the plunge.

For if we as a society don't pause and take stock of the kind of world we want our children to grow up in, and what we hope they'll try to do about it, we may find all our best intentions crumbling, along with civilization itself, like a wall made of sand and rock, but no cement.

Here again, then, lies a natural focus for the energies of Cities of Light. For the whole purpose of such communities cannot but be to focus the creative energies of their members in a search for new solutions to old problems. Clearly, if the members of an intentional community marry and raise families, they will want also to develop schools for their children. Equally obviously, one of the priorities of such communities will be to develop schools that explore ways of teaching moral and spiritual values along with French, physics, and algebra.

The modern age is addicted to factual information. By "addiction" I mean that the fascination has reached abnormal proportions. It is necessary for us, then, to emphasize that facts by themselves cannot bestow wisdom. A blizzard of unsifted information can only confuse the mind. It will offer it no sense of direction, nor any knowledge of where one might go to get out of the storm.

It is better to have at one's command a little well-digested knowledge than to go about with such a head full of information that all one gets for his trouble is more pain—the severe cramps, in fact, of intellectual indigestion.

We forget, in all our huffing and puffing as we rush headlong down the stairs, that the discovery of some new fact concerning a galaxy trillions of light years away has very little actual bearing on our lives here on earth. The knowledge, on the other hand, of how to get along with others, and how to be happy, has a great deal of bearing. What goes on out there in the universe is fascinating, no doubt. Even so, the responsibility for running the universe is not mankind's.

Nor, thank God, is the burden. A question of much more immediate importance to mankind is what goes on in our own lives, and not what happens "out there" in space.

I don't at all mean to halt the investigations of science. Even if we should derive no useful information at all from all its probing, a constant need of mankind's is being deeply satisfied by modern scientific discoveries. For curiosity about this great universe of which we are a part is one of mankind's abiding characteristics. Scientists, moreover, aver that some of the most abstract-seeming studies in physics and astronomy often end up proving of great practical benefit to mankind.

No, all I'm saying is that all this research must not be allowed to distort our sense of proportion.

Our position today is similar to that of people five hundred years ago, when the discovery of the New World was announced. The adventure of exploration seized people's imaginations then, even as the adventure of scientific research has fired our imaginations today. News of new lands, of unimaginable cities, and of strange people and customs spread like wildfire through the Old World. New foods, such as corn, and new practices, such as the smoking of tobacco, filled people with a constant sense of wonder.

The conquistadores in the New World stole its wealth for Spain. England's adventurers, on the other hand, brought back with them dreams of colonizing and developing the New World. Many people set aside for a time the heavy considerations of moral and spiritual values. But did moral law comply by ignoring them? Far from it!

Spain soon fell from her position as a great power. And it was during that same period that England's era of prosperity began. Even now, centuries later, South America has yet to achieve political equilibrium and economic prosperity. North America's prosperity, on the other hand, is legendary throughout the world.

Spiritual and moral laws, similar to action and reaction in physics, never changed, though the excitement of that era made people on the whole lose sight of them for a time—an oversight, indeed, the reverberations of which seem to have continued to this day.

These values haven't changed in our own age, either. The excitement of scientific discovery has captured men's imaginations, but the laws that rule human conduct remain unalterable.

There is no point in blaming anyone for the present trend. Indeed, it is completely understandable that our century should have been swept away by the great adventure of modern times, and why people caught up in the adventure have not given very much thought to the "Old World" of traditional values.

It is even forgivable that people should have come back glowing from their scientific research to announce that the old values have been overthrown. All that this eloquence really reveals is the natural ebullience of human nature under the intoxication of new discoveries. If we weren't made like that, we wouldn't be human. Nor, probably, would we ever accomplish anything worthwhile in life. As Ralph Waldo Emerson put it, "Nothing great was ever achieved without enthusiasm."

And the scientific thinkers are right: The vastness of the universe makes mankind seem almost absurdly unimportant in the greater scheme of things. The antiquity even of life on our little planet makes man's place in the great eons of earth-time seem insignificant. Even the way the human race is believed to have appeared on earth—as a mere accident of life's long struggle for survival—is claimed by many to have robbed mankind of special worth. (Though the way evolution has always placed a premium on intelligence might suggest to people's minds that the end of the story was predetermined, whatever twists the plot took along the way.)

It is almost a game with these new adventurers of science, to tease the rest of us stay-at-homes for our preoccupation with the paltry human species.

The trouble is that games played with ideas are not the same thing as games played with colored balls. Ideas have consequences. As has been stressed repeatedly in this book, the materialistic philosophy of this age threatens seriously to destroy our civilization. And if it does that, I can imagine scientists looking up from their test tubes, blinking, and exclaiming, "But where will our funding come from?"

The defenders of traditional values, understandably, want a confrontation with those thinkers whose aim has been to define all moral and spiritual values as matters of mere "convenience"—in effect, throwing them out the window (though they have nicer ways of putting it). Unfortunately, the people who want to defend values, and those other people whose thoughts are elsewhere, don't seem capable of talking the same language.

The traditionalists complain that science, and the thinkers whose philosophies have sprung out of the findings of science, have undermined traditional beliefs. What kind of argument is that? *Of course* science has undermined traditional beliefs! It has been doing its best for centuries to do exactly that.

It's as if the people of the Old World were to confront the Walter Raleighs of their age with the complaint, "But— you've left your villages!"

The great adventure of science has been based on its demonstration of the need for testing every belief. If the only argument the traditionalists can mount against science is to say, "But here's a body of untested beliefs that you mustn't touch," all they can possibly accomplish is to strengthen the hands of those who insist that moral values are without any foundation except that of convenience. Eventually, with this weak argument, the traditionalists will completely destroy their own position.

The weakness of the traditionalist position is that it assumes the purpose behind all moral and spiritual law to be God's will, rather than human welfare. Traditionalists teach moral values as God's *Commandments* to man.

Mankind, living under this cloud of divine obligation, has always tended to think that the Lord was only trying to make things difficult for all of us. (Indeed, one detects a certain glee in the way people have used science to justify their rejection of the Commandments.)

The problem, as in the confrontation between materialists and religious people, is not that religion is at fault, but only that church dogmas were designed to meet the spiritual challenges of an earlier age. No dogma could ever stand in place of the truths it attempts to define, just as no mere definition of a tree could ever produce leaves.

What is needed today is a new approach to old dogmas. To accomplish this, Jesus himself pointed the way! His saying, on the subject of one of the Ten Commandments, was, "The Sabbath was made for man, and not man for the Sabbath." Clearly, the point he was making was that the Commandments were laws that related to human well-being. They had nothing to do with ordering man to be blindly obedient to God's will.

If a person eats red-hot nails, he will injure his body irreparably. Since everyone knows he can't eat hot nails, no one has bothered to write dietary rules proscribing such behavior. There are other laws of human nature, however, that are not so immediately obvious. Laws have had to be written to draw people's attention to them.

The so-called "Commandments" are really only wise guidelines, intended to help mankind to behave in such a way as to promote his own well-being.

The moral traditionalists, by trying to remove moral values from intelligent investigation, have only played into the hands of the materialists, who walk away from the debate saying, "Our opponents never showed up." A completely different approach is needed. For if indeed traditional values have the importance that traditional-ists claim, then they must be able to stand serenely under the glare of the most insistent investigation. As Yogananda once said, "Truth is not afraid of questions."

The time has come for man to get back to his proper study, which, as Alexander Pope said, is man.

The explorers of the New World returned with priceless discoveries that benefited everyone at home. It is time now

for mankind to turn the scientific method upon the important issue of man, and of those moral and spiritual values
which can serve him in his search for inner fulfillment.

And it is time also to pursue this investigation in the
schools, as part of the process of education.

It is time to approach materialism itself from a fresh point
of view. Paramhansa Yogananda, as we saw earlier, offered
an amazingly simple answer to materialists who claimed
that consciousness—the manifestations of which are
observable in the rocks—exists only as an aspect of inanimate matter. Traditional dogma has no answer to this claim;
it has always said that matter is inert. Yogananda, however,
replied, "No, what this means is that matter, too, is conscious,
however dimly so."

Yogananda also gave this simple suggestion on the subject
of values: that the effect of moral values on human nature
be tested, as if in the laboratory, by observing their actual
effects on people. He suggested that communities be seen
as opportunities for conducting such observations—as,
indeed, we have had ample opportunity to do at Ananda.

He also suggested that moral education in the schools be
approached in the same way. This is the approach we take

in our schools at Ananda. We have found that it works wonderfully.

Teachers and parents may complain that if too much time is spent in teaching children these things, they'll get left behind in the race to acquire that information which will fit them to compete in the job market after they leave school. Let us look at the question this way:

Two people decide to learn to ski. One of them, impatient to master the slopes, goes straight to the steepest of them and sets off downhill. Falling constantly, he covers a lot of ground, but most of it on his back, sides, and stomach.

The other beginner decides he must first learn to master the movements of his own body. Carefully, he learns first how to turn, how to snowplow, how to stop.

Of these two skiers, which is the more likely to be the first to master the slopes?

The better that children can be taught to concentrate, to increase their awareness, and to channel negative emotions into constructive outlets, the more effectively they'll be able to handle all the factual information they're taught in school also.

There is also another important dimension that needs to be introduced into the schools. Children are made to study the composition of the atom. The most important question of all, however—essential, in fact, because it touches everyone at the very core of his being—is this: "How can one find happiness?" Schools, Yogananda said, should above all be treated as laboratories for the solving of this most basic of human questions.

Cities of Light, because they are dedicated to finding a better way of living, are the natural soil in which to conduct such experiments. The schools in such communities can prove to be—*and have already proved to be*—among the most exciting and rewarding aspects of living in Crystal Clarity.

Crystal Clarity in the Arts

Chapter eleven

The concept of Cities of Light might be likened to a great wheel, the hub of which is the central concept itself: a life lived in Crystal Clarity, in expanded, divine awareness. The spokes of the wheel, radiating outward from the hub, are the outward expressions of that consciousness of Crystal Clarity. And the rim represents the unity of those outward expressions in cooperative, mutually supportive activity. The rim, then, denotes the community's life as a totality, both as it revolves upon itself and as it touches the rest of the world.

The spokes that radiate outward from this hub include the expression of Crystal Clarity in business, in home building, in family life, in government and leadership, in marriage, in education, and, indeed, in every phase of life. There is no aspect of human existence that cannot receive fresh clarity and vitality, when we apply to it these central principles.

One of the most fertile fields for applying Crystal Clarity is the arts. For men are led more surely through the arts than through philosophy. Philosophy touches only their minds, but the arts involve also their feelings. The arts affect people's lives as outward expressions of their ideas. Indeed, if the arts are broad enough in their vision, they can touch also the soul.

New ideas almost always begin as philosophy. At this stage they may be read and discussed by few—even as, in science, Einstein was first discussed by only a handful of other scientists, and understood by even fewer. Creative artists (composers, writers, and others who express themselves creatively) are usually closer to new waves of thought than the general mass of people. Few artists are philosophers themselves, but they enjoy the stimulation of new ideas, and tend to become the popularizers of those ideas. Thus, through the arts new concepts reach out and actually touch the common man.

The arts, therefore, are in one sense the most important expression that can come out of the vision of Crystal Clarity. For people may lecture and theorize abstractly, even enthusiastically, without really moving even themselves to practical action. The way to make a new idea really one's own is to live it. And the best way of living it, short of embracing it wholly, is to experience it vicariously through some form of artistic expression.

A novel that describes people living in a new state of awareness can give the reader almost the feeling that he, too, shares in that awareness. A painting that describes social injustice can bring the reality of that injustice more vividly to the heart and mind than any mere lecture on the subject. Music, too, can stir an experience of new states of awareness.

If there is one thing, then, that Cities of Light ought to focus on, it is the question of how to express their philosophy through the arts. Probably only after they've succeeded in expressing their ideals and their state of consciousness through some aspect of the arts will people generally come to appreciate what they represent.

The only influence greater than the arts in its potential for inspiring people is direct, inner religious experience. This doesn't mean fanaticism or religious dogmatism, but rather some actual experience of inner, divine blessing. People who have been so blessed find themselves transformed from inside, and not merely superficially, through their emotions and imaginations. Such an inner change is much greater and more enduring than any that is effected from without, through the arts.

Cities of Light need, as I've said repeatedly, to be developed as a new kind of monastic order; otherwise, they will not succeed. Communities that have a spiritual base will naturally be able to touch people on a soul-level. The more they themselves experience of God's presence in their lives, the better they will be able to share with others something vital and valid.

In addition to touching others directly on a soul level, however, they can touch people also, and perhaps reach many more people, through the arts. The arts, therefore, will always be one of the best possible ways for communities to reach out to others. They will also remain an important way for a community to clarify its own directions.

Members of the community that have a talent for artistic expression should be encouraged to paint, write, compose music, sing, write plays and act in them, create spiritually inspiring dances, and carve in stone or cast in iron the great, central ideas that have ever uplifted the human race, and that will ever continue to do so.

Artistic expression in this century expresses the negative philosophy of our times. This philosophy is—even self-vauntingly so—materialistic, ego-centered, iconoclastic and contemptuous of high ideals. It is atheistic, and filled with affirmations of meaninglessness and despair. New art forms are waiting to express a more exalted philosophy.

Such forms can only come out of the sort of new vision that Cities of Light can provide. For it would not be possible to bring new insights into being while surrounded by old influences, and by the daily repetition of old clichés.

An example of this impossibility is the new wave of Christian music. It represents a desperate attempt to reawaken devotion to the teachings of the Bible by setting high sentiments to the popular beat of rock music. Rock and roll, however, is a music form that places heavy stress on the ego. The singers of this new Christian music actually go to the lengths of appearing dressed fantastically in sequins, in imitation of popular rock stars. Their dress, their music, their very comportment all seem to shout, "Look at me!" Only the words they sing are different, and what good does it do to sing, "Love Jesus!" if everything else about you is pleading, "Yeah, yeah, but love me, too!"

The dilemma is the same for actors. What plays are there for them to act in that represent truly the deep spiritual needs of our times? None, with which I am familiar, anyway.

It is necessary first to produce artistic forms that will express a consciousness of Crystal Clarity. Such creations will then naturally find expression through the interpretive arts.

Crystal Clarity as it applies to the arts should involve communication with all things as manifestations of consciousness. It should mean seeing them as expressions *in*, and not only *of*, Crystal Clarity. It should entail a reaching out to relate to broader realities than one's own, so that the work one is creating will suggest a greater sphere of reality than it expresses overtly.

The essence of good taste, always, is understatement. A good painting will suggest moods and feelings without actually labeling them. In its very suggestion it implies recognition that there is a certain consciousness present in its subject—even if the subject be a flower, a rock, or a stream.

Crystal Clarity in the arts means art that communicates—and that communicates not only with the people who, so the artist hopes, will enjoy his work, but also with his subject. If nothing else, Crystal Clarity can be his means of opening up new layers of sensitivity within himself.

If, however, the teaching is true that matter expresses consciousness, however dim the degree of consciousness expressed, then the arts afford man a means of actually expanding his consciousness into a greater, *conscious*, reality.

At Ananda, artistic inspiration has found outlet through new forms of expression in music, songs, poetry, stories, photography, painting, and simply through the effort, manifested everywhere, to create beautiful homes and a harmonious environment. The constant effort of the community members is to serve, on every level possible, as channels of Crystal Clarity.

Perhaps it would be good to include, as an example of the arts, a life lived in Crystal Clarity. For is not this the highest purpose of the arts—that they help us to live our own lives more consciously?

Crystal Clarity and the New Age

Chapter twelve

That we are living in a new age seems obvious. Toward the end of the last century, it was seriously proposed in Congress that the Patent Office be closed, inasmuch as everything that could possibly be invented had been invented already. Everything, virtually, that we identify with modern civilization has been invented since that time.

We seem, moreover, to be only at the beginning of whatever wave of discovery is presently sweeping us into the future. Science's new insights into the nature of matter have caused a revolution in thought. Matter is no longer seen as solid. Indeed, it is composed almost entirely of space. The atoms whirl through this space like stellar systems, and are as remote from one another, relatively speaking. Even the atom is not the last word on what matter is. For matter has been discovered to be energy. As such, it lacks even the flimsy substance of atomic structure.

These scientifically demonstrated realities have had a profound impact on human thought. That most of the conclusions drawn so far have seemed detrimental to mankind's spiritual vision has naturally caused a reaction among those who hold such a vision.

Many people have denounced the very concept of a new age, as though it were possible to turn back the clock to Biblical times. All such endeavors are futile. A new age is upon us, whether we like it or not. It is up to us to see whether we can't make good sense out of it, rather than bad sense, and in any case whether we can't make *some* sense of it.

It seems almost inevitable that the dissolution of our conception of matter as a changeless, solid reality is going to affect permanently how we view the seemingly fixed realities in our lives. The effect of new scientific discoveries has been felt in the realm of ideas. It is our ideas about reality, therefore, that will have to undergo the most radical transformation.

Traditionally, people have tried to solidify their concepts by enshrining them in institutions, or by freezing them in fixed dogmas and definitions. Inevitably, in this scientific age, institutionalism will take a beating. Definitions will be tested, and continually retested, by the yardstick of living experience. Old, rigid rules of behavior will be relaxed in favor of a more tolerant and compassionate view of man's efforts to improve himself. Creativity will be given more freedom of self-expression. Old dogmas will be reinterpreted to include a broader view of reality. Dogmatism, probably, with its mere definitions of truth, will to a great extent be replaced by a growing emphasis on the direct experience of God.

None of these consequences, expressed thus, seems bad. Rather, they all seem part of the great adventure of adjusting our understanding of things to the discovery of whole new continents of reality. Personally, I find the prospect thrilling and exciting.

Many of the people, however, who claim to speak on behalf of a "New Age" do so with a certain blustering presumption. They are as blind to the higher potentials of the new age as those who insist that the new age be abolished. Their presumption lies in the thought that mankind, by his efforts alone, will bring the new age into existence. And their blindness is manifested in the emphasis they place on egoic, rather than on divine, values.

The dream of too many people in the so-called "New Age Movement" is of a heaven on earth without God, without humility, and without devotion—a "heaven" in which mankind reigns supreme, holding in his own puny hands the power of the universe. There is something seriously wrong with this philosophy. It marks, however, the main direction taken by many people in "New Thought," or by those who are "into consciousness"—from Westerners who embrace oriental religions without understanding them, to those Christians who devote all their energy to "manifesting" health and wealth, and finally to those dreamers who think they can create the perfect society through merely material systems.

If the material universe is, as Yogananda claimed, composed of consciousness, and not merely of energy, then the whole scene shifts from a human to a divine event. In this case, the new age is not man's opportunity to become divinely powerful, but God's opportunity to express Himself more perfectly through man.

In this context, we see even more forcefully presented to us the need for Cities of Light. We are living in a new age indeed, and the principal influence of this new age lies already in the realm of ideas. The most important challenge facing us, then, is to clarify our ideas—about life, about mankind, about society, leadership, marriage, education, the arts—about God, and about our relation to the world and to the greater universe. Is there any level of thought that hasn't been affected by the discoveries of science?

Cities of Light can change the depressing modern trend to assume only the worst from everything science tells of the nature of reality. People of good will need to redefine their lives, and to bring them into attunement once again with God, that they may understand with Crystal Clarity the new insights He is sending into the minds of men.

An example of my meaning may be taken from the Women's Liberation movement. People seldom realize the extent to which their new ideas are influenced from above. When a new wave of consciousness ripples across the world, people seize it as their own, attach their own names to it, and campaign up and down the land, crying, "Listen to what I have to say!" In the process, they confuse what was at first sent into the world as a loving, divine inspiration for the welfare of all mankind.

There is certainly a need for more feminine influence in the world—for more compassion, more receptivity, more love. It is right that this feminine energy be given equal importance with the traditionally more dominant masculine energies of impersonal justice, conquest, and reason. It is an obvious requirement of this rightness that equality between the two energies manifest itself on every outward level of activity: in jobs, in politics, in the home.

It is a beautiful manifestation of our age. It has resulted in a much more sensitive attitude toward our environment; in talk of cooperation, instead of competition, between nations and between groups of people; in a wish to improve the quality of life, instead of striving forever to "get ahead."

Why, then, have so many women—and men, too, for that matter—made an ugly scene of it? By all their anger, their egotism, their aggressiveness, they distort the divine vibrations and permit only a few drops of grace to fall, when God is offering to create a whole lake.

The same is true with every aspect of the new age. We need to attune ourselves to its rays in humility and love, and not go striding about with banners proclaiming, "*We* are the New Age!" Could a flute play a single note, without the flutist?

Cities of Light offer a concept whereby devoted men and women can concentrate their energies in attunement with God's energies, and see how best they can serve as channels of His light to all the earth.

The Expanding Light

Chapter thirteen

On earth today there is a great darkness. Like an evil cloud, it is spreading into every land. Many well-meaning, intelligent people—people also in positions of worldly power and authority—find themselves caught in its clinging mists, unable to trace their way back into the light.

No person of good will wants to see the world caught in the grip of authoritarianism, suppression, cynicism, or the total loss of all those values which give dignity and worth to the human race. Yet many good people nowadays find themselves seduced by dreams that can have no other consequences than these. Influences of which these people haven't even any knowledge cloud their reasoning, and cause them to embrace, even enthusiastically, lines of reasoning that can have no other end than the destruction of civilization.

In country after country, the lights of freedom are being extinguished. In schools everywhere, concepts are being taught that justify darkness in the name of scientific truth, and then name that truth, "Light." Well-meaning teachers, swayed by such simplistic slogans as "compassion," pay lip service to freedom while they stress to their students the superior merits of systems that substitute security for freedom, and governmental controls for the unpredictability and uncertainty of free enterprise.

Intelligent people are seduced by appeals to their intellectual brilliance: "See the folly of allowing the masses to make important decisions for themselves!" The masses are seduced by appeals to the great, mysterious power emanating from that vague entity, "The People." Fair-minded people are seduced by appeals to their humility: "Who are we, after all, to claim that we are always right, and they, always wrong?" Idealists are seduced by appeals to their dreams of a better world—dreams as undefined and unclear as their own ideals. Peace-loving people are seduced by appeals to their desire to avoid war as the greatest evil possible to man.

Everyone is blinded to the truth.

Can't people *see* the darkness? They laugh, in their scientific "enlightenment," at the concept of Satan, and see not how deeply enmeshed they themselves are in the tentacles of darkness that are reaching across the world.

Materialism is no armchair philosophy any more. It is not an interesting theory to play with at dinner parties, when the conversation gets dull. It is much more than an idea. It has assumed the dimensions of a powerful and spreading thought form, reaching into the minds of men everywhere, giving them what look like good reasons to believe that only matter is real; that man's lower nature is what he really is, and that his ideals are but his cowardly attempt to avoid facing that reality; that life is eternally meaningless; that wisdom is a dream, love is a dream, consciousness itself is only a delusion; that religion is the worst lie ever perpetrated on the human race; that the highest wisdom is to live only for oneself, to get everything one can for oneself, to enjoy oneself at the expense of others, and to realize that morality is only a placebo to keep the masses under control.

Geologists have a way of smiling at human presumption as they describe the vast eons of geologic time. Materialists, similarly, have a way of smiling, and for much the same reason, as they describe the meaninglessness of life, and the insignificance of human striving. It gives *them* a sense of significance to describe man's insignificance. It makes them feel intelligent to describe the unreality of man's intelligence.

Why need it surprise us that educated people plunge with so much dedication into plotting their own destruction? Under the justification of materialism, even the most desperate behavior is conceivable.

One of the supreme ironies of this religion of anti-values is the large numbers of Christian priests and ministers it has converted—actually, and unbelievably, *in the name of Christ*. Their seduction has been a step-by-step process: first, the thought that mystical love for God is not relevant to the heart that is filled with compassion for suffering mankind; second, that when people ache with hunger they need food, not consolation; third, that their material needs are more important than the needs of their souls; fourth, that material needs are the *real* needs, and soul needs—well, who knows? Thus, step by step, matter, not spirit, becomes bedrock reality for these priests—and all in the name of Jesus! They embrace materialism, then find themselves forced to follow its broad highway, looking always for an exit, but finding none.

Satan's greatest triumph, as has been well said, lies in his success in persuading people that he doesn't exist. They visualize him as a sinister, creeping, caped villain with horns, cloven hooves, and a tail, then compare that image with the grandeur of the galaxies, and laugh.

But what about another image: great clouds of mental darkness that sweep the universe, looking for minds that are open to—nay, that invite—their influence. Imagine a planet where vast numbers of its inhabitants have already been swayed to believe that matter is the ultimate reality. That is exactly the aim of those great forces of evil—to drive toward unawareness every thought that reaches upward hopefully to embrace the light; to persuade souls that light is an illusion, that love and joy do not exist, and that, throughout creation, all is darkness, dull matter, and unconsciousness.

If there be joy in hell, must there not be nightly celebrations now, at the growing contempt in people's minds for their own souls?

Clouds of darkness range the universe. But so also, fortunately, do great clouds of light. Forces of darkness and of light vie constantly for victory in human hearts—and not in people on this planet only, but on peopled planets every-where in space. Those powers respond as they are called. Man has the power to reject the one, and to invite the other.

Darkness cannot be banished from a room by beating at it with a stick. Evil is not discouraged by men's hatred of it. Indeed, by concentration on it they increase its hold on them. By hatred of it, they invite its entry by back doors of their consciousness. Evil thrives on hatred, even when what is hated is evil itself.

Darkness can be banished only thus: by turning on the light.

The true warfare of modern times is that which rages between darkness and light. The truest weapon in this warfare, for those who would help the light to win, is the offering of one's heart and soul to be a channel of the light. The victory may need guns as well, if nations go to war. God's way is not passivity. But love is the divine force. And also faith. And light.

The angels, too, have bent down to earth to rescue man. Great waves of light and inspiration are pouring down upon the great sea of human minds, seeking those whom they can uplift in grace.

Satan's best hope, with those who would serve the light, is to send them the suggestion: "*Yours* is the responsibility. Why look to God? Why look to any greater power than your own? Why look to others to inspire you? All are but men, like you. From you alone can come the power to do what little good is given you to do."

The voice of God within us calls, however, and says, "Poor, puny man! Who are you to lift a stone, a leaf, a grain of sand without My power? Mine is the power, never thine! True strength comes to you, the more you open up your heart and mind to be a channel for My light. When you help others, it is My help that you transmit to them. When you comfort them, it is My comfort you convey. When you give them love, know that it is My love that fills your heart and touches them. Be consciously in tune with Me, if you would do that great good which I Myself would give to you to do."

Thus, while darkness spreads, so also does the light. Those who choose neither light nor darkness are drawn down beneath the waters, for it takes strength to fly. But those who choose to rise into the light are given wings. Many there are, moreover, who, having seen the cloud of evil as it spreads across the earth, tremble not, but cry with love to the heavens, "I believe in light!" And with their cry, a ray of light is sent down to them, and they begin to rise.

Great saints are examples of transmitters of such rays of light. So also, and more greatly, are those masters who were born for the upliftment of mankind.

One such line of masters included Paramhansa Yogananda, and those before him, who sent him to the West. He brought with Him a great wave of God's light, and no ray merely. Thousands, receiving into their lives the divine power for which he served as a channel, have found the darkness of their egos receding from their minds, and the love of God entering in, and filling them.

Humility was Yogananda's hallmark. More than any man I've ever met, he gave all glory to God, seeking none for himself. What he sought to inspire in everyone was the awareness that God resides in all; that each must seek Him, not outwardly in forms, but deeply within, in the silence of inner communion.

Ananda's success, as its members well know, is due to God's grace alone, and to the divine light that Yogananda, who empowered this work, has channeled from Infinity to this humble band, sincerely bent on loving God more perfectly, and on serving Him in their turn, as He enables them, as channels of His light.

Our work of public service at Ananda is called "The Expanding Light." People come here from all over the world for classes, divine worship, and simply to rejoice with us together in God's light and love. Daily services are held here, and meditations, and singing in deep joy.

Come, if you can, and share with us. Together, let us serve the light. Together, let us ask that it descend in power and mounting glory, until the clouds of darkness roll away from the face of earth, and the sunlight of God's joy once more brings harmony to man.

Channeling the Light

Chapter fourteen

The powers of darkness are attracted to those places where darkness, squalor, and confusion reign. The powers of light, on the other hand, are attracted wherever there is light, and love, and Crystal Clarity.

To draw God's light down to earth, pure hearts are needed—devotees whose will is to live in light. Even as squalor attracts negative energies, however, so outward harmony and beauty attract Godly energies. Man cannot create heaven on this earth, for heaven is in God. But his duty is to *reflect* heaven in all he does, and in all that he creates.

It isn't that God comes only where beauty is manifested outwardly. Those, however, who serve as channels of His light feel naturally inspired to channel that light into all aspects of their lives, as well as outwardly to their environments.

Cities of Light will always, in time, become places of simple beauty outwardly, as well as places of great inward harmony.

Ananda's effort to attune itself to God's light includes daily chanting, prayer, and meditation. We practice daily also the technique of Kriya Yoga, which is the holy science that Paramhansa Yogananda brought to the West. Kriya Yoga helps people to bring themselves into alignment and harmony with the downward flow of God's grace.

We meditate individually, as well as in company with others. Whether alone or in groups, we try to unite our spirits with those of the other members, and with all those, everywhere, who are seeking to serve as channels for God's light.

In everything we do, we pray to God to enlighten and inspire us. At the same time, we keep in mind that divine inspiration comes not only in silent prayer, but also in the "prayer" of labor that is lovingly offered up to Him. As Yogananda taught us to do, we pray, "Lord, I will reason, I will will, I will act, but guide Thou my reason, will, and activity to the right path in everything."

In keeping with our belief that outward harmony helps to draw divine blessings down to earth, we express our inner experience of God's presence outwardly as well, through simple, beautiful, and uplifting ceremonies. One of these has been excerpted already in this book—the Wedding Ceremony.

Others include Baptism, in which we welcome the newborn soul into our midst, and invite it to remember always that its highest duty is to seek truth and God, and to include the welfare of others in its own welfare. At this ceremony other children in the community dance around the baby, welcoming it as they sing:

> Friend, we bid you welcome!
>
> Welcome!
>
> Welcome!
>
> All that we learn,
>
> We'll share with you.
>
> That way, we'll grow together!

Ceremonies include one also for when people leave this world. There is a ceremony of healing, one for inner purification, and another to help us to achieve higher attunement. Vows of dedication are said by the members. Vows of self-offering in service are said by those receiving ordination as ministers. And there is the ceremony of initiation into the sacred art and science of Kriya Yoga.

One of our most important ceremonies is the Festival of Light, during which God's light is invoked to flow down to earth, and into the hearts of worshipers both present and afar, through the channels of Jesus Christ, our line of masters, and the great saints of all religions.

In this service, the minister reminds the congregation of the blessings that are received as a result of living in God's light (hence the name, "Festival of Light").

Nothing, perhaps, could so clearly convey our sense of inspiration in the life we lead as excerpts from that ceremony. Let me quote parts of it here.

A FESTIVAL OF LIGHT

(Minister)

> Let us lift up our hearts in a festival of light.
>
> The essence of this ceremony has been passed down from ancient times.
>
> O waves that we are on the bosom of the Infinite Sea, joyfully together let us celebrate our own greater reality. For now by God's grace our redemption is at hand. The divine light, returning anew to earth, has given us power, as the Holy Bible proclaims, "to become the sons of God."

Into our hands have been delivered the sacred keys of awakening.

Abundant now is our hope!

The Lord, through the Bhagavad Gita, promised: "Even the worst of sinners, by steadfast meditation on Me, speedily comes to Me." Again in that holy scripture He declared, "Even a little practice of this inward religion will free one from dire fears and colossal sufferings."

And whereas suffering and sorrow, in the past, was the coin of man's redemption, for us now the payment has been exchanged for calm acceptance and joy. Thus may we understand that pain is the fruit of self-love, whereas joy is the fruit of love for God.

From sun and moon and all the stars,

From glistening seas, high mountains, desert solitudes, and vast, fruitful plains,

And from the hearts of mankind, and of creatures everywhere,

Goes up in wordless yearning a prayer for redemption:

O Mighty Source of all that is:

From sorrow, lead us to everlasting joy;

From darkness, lead us to infinite light;

From death, lead us to immortality! . . .

(A long section follows, then the following words are spoken:)

The forming of stars and moons and planets,

Of galaxies revolving on the tides of space,

Of drifting continents, upheaving mountains,

Snowy wastes and dark, silent ocean deeps

Had but this for its design: the birth of life,

And, with life's birth, the dawn of self-awareness:

Passage through dim corridors of waking consciousness

To emerge at last into infinite light—

Into perfect joy!

O Children of Light, forsake the darkness!

Know that, forever, you and He are one!

(The ceremony continues, taking the devotee ever deeper in the thought of attunement, and in gratitude to God and to the line of masters for the grace of light.)

Thus, may all souls feel, and know, the power of God in their lives. For He is, as the scriptures say, "supremely relishable." God's joy is the only true joy in life. For the soul, there is no other reality.

Guidelines for Conduct

Chapter fifteen

The guidelines for conduct for members of Ananda have evolved out of many years of experience. They merit study by any group desirous of creating a City of Light, and certainly make required reading by any group aspiring to become an Ananda community.

What follow here are excerpts, only, of the complete guidelines, which are available also to interested persons.

MEMBERSHIP DEFINED

Who are we? What is Ananda?

We have come together as a community of spirit. Our primary purpose is to find God, by meditation, and by service to God through our fellowman.

Our lives are offered in openness as channels to the Divine Light, in order that, by loving cooperation with God's grace, His light, through us, may expand its influence on earth.

Our goal is not to create heaven on earth, but only to reflect it here. For we realize that matter can never be more than an imperfect medium for the expression of divine realities.

In service to others, our ideal is to serve God equally in all.

In meditation, our ideal is to set aside the ego and to allow the divine consciousness to penetrate into every corner of our beings.

MONASTIC COMMUNITY LIFE DEFINED

We are dedicated to living in divine unity as an expanded family, under the guidance and inspiration that has been channeled to us from our one Father-Mother, God. The homes we live in may be many and separate. Our greater home, however, unites us in God's Spirit. This greater home embraces more than the physical property of Ananda. It includes also that special ray of the Divine Light in which we all strive to live, and which we try to express in our lives, wherever our physical bodies may be located.

Life in a monastic order is, in a sense, like marriage. For whatever one member does affects everyone. Whatever hurts one is hurtful to all. And whatever benefits one accrues to the benefit of all. As one member develops spiritually, all members develop. And as one diminishes, all thereby diminish to some extent also.

Such a life, then, cannot reasonably entail a strong affirmation of personal freedom and independence. In any personal decision, the welfare of all should be taken into account. In every member's search for personal happiness, the happiness of the other members should be considered.

Ananda members should therefore work together always in a spirit of unity, and never with selfishness or pride. They should endeavor to help one another on every level: physically, mentally, and spiritually. The help they offer, moreover, should never be imposed. It should be tendered with respect and love, rather, in full awareness that a sincere offer confers no obligation.

No major decision in any member's life should be made without consulting his larger spiritual family, or an appointed representative or group of representatives of that family. "Loyalty," Paramhansa Yogananda often said, "is the first law of God." He spoke strongly concerning the opposite quality to loyalty. "Treachery," he told his disciples, "is the greatest sin before God. For moral sins are committed in weakness, under the influence of past habit. But treachery is deliberate."

Let every member take his words on this subject to heart, and meditate on how they may apply to his life in all its aspects. For both loyalty and treachery have their reality first, not in action, but in the mind.

It is not disloyal to disagree. It is disloyal, however, to take one's disagreement to those who are not in a position to influence matters for the better, or who cannot at least help one to achieve greater clarity on the subject.

It is not necessarily a sign of loyalty, on the other hand, merely to agree—if, for example, one's agreement is with what he inwardly perceives as an error. It is a sign of loyalty, however, to support one's spiritual family regardless of one's disagreement with some of its directions, provided those directions constitute no major threat to what should always be the member's highest loyalty: his commitment to God.

It is not loyal, in the name of "fairness" and "objectivity," to withhold support from community decisions, once these decisions have been agreed upon. Nor is it loyal, in the name of "open-mindedness," to hold oneself aloof in such matters as if claiming to represent some higher wisdom that is not being accepted. Perfection cannot be achieved here on earth. Is it not wrong, then, to make such minor imperfections as one may find, or imagine one has found, in his chosen spiritual family his excuse for withholding mental support?

Does one, for instance, for the imperfections that he may observe in his own mother, hold himself aloof from her? She is his mother, after all, her human shortcomings notwithstanding. When there is love, a person's deepest awareness will always be of the causes for unity, not for disunity.

Members, wherever they may go, should see themselves as channels of God and of the ray of divine light that is expressed through Ananda. They should behave themselves accordingly—joyfully, of course, but never with abandon, and always with God-remembrance. They ought to strive consciously to project their inner light, so that that light— which is to say, God's light, through them—may touch, on some level, everyone they meet.

SPIRITUAL PRACTICES

The members of Ananda should meditate daily, and practice regularly their techniques of meditation and energization. . . .

Members should participate in the spiritual life of the community, including scheduled group meditations. . . . Their attendance also at divine services should be regular. . . .

Every member should try to take one or more weeks of seclusion every year, during which time he devotes himself intensely to meditation, silence, and practicing the presence of God. In addition, he should try every week to set aside one day for deeper absorption in God-keeping silence, if possible, and meditating longer hours than normal.

HOME LIFE

Ananda Sevakas should not view their homes in normal worldly terms, as their "castle," but as temples of God. They should fill them with godly vibrations, with devotion and joy.

Interaction with others within the home should be based not on egoic familiarity, but on mutual respect, supportiveness, and love. Life's longer rhythms should be emphasized in every familial and friendly relationship, and the frictions of the moment, if any, seen always in a more enduring context.

Every home ought to have a separate room—or some area set apart, and preferably screened off, in a larger room—as the family's private meditation chapelchapel. . . . Strictly prohibited to Ananda

Strictly prohibited to all Ananda members is the use, both on and off the property, of hallucinogenic drugs and alcoholic beverages. An exception to the proscription against alcoholic beverages may be allowed for medicinal needs.

Dietary rules are not strict, and are left up to the individual member. It is assumed, however, that an Ananda member will voluntarily confine his diet to those foods which, in the teachings of Paramhansa Yogananda, are recommended for the refinement of a person's spiritual awareness. awareness. . . . The member should look upon his body as the temple of God, and treat it accordingly. He should give it proper daily exercise, but should not make exercise the center of his life. He should not drug his mind and body with too much sleep, nor yet, in a spirit of fanatical dedication, deprive himself of needed sleep. In every way he should treat his body with respect and care, without over-indulging it—much as he would treat a friend.

A couple should look upon each other, also, as temples of God. Every aspect of their relationship should be touched with "other"-consciousness—that is to say, with the feeling that they are relating to each other not only on a human level, but inwardly, in spirit.

WORK IS SERVICE

All Ananda members should view whatever gainful employment they seek as a service, never merely as work. The mere thought of hard work, indeed, often drains a person's energies, whereas joyful, willing service opens inner floodgates to a boundless supply of energy.

Expansive service, moreover, in God's name, is much more spiritually regenerating than that constricted service, motivated by human feelings, which people commonly offer to the few whom they consider their own. Even those closest to them should be served, rather, with the thought that, through them, one is serving God. The employment sought by members should be in keeping with Ananda's ideals; it should not be selected from financial motives alone. Above all, it should be approached in the light of the opportunities it affords for serving others in a divine way.

Ananda members are free both to create their own businesses and to import businesses from outside the community. They are free, as well, to pursue their own personal careers. No gainful activity should be admitted into Ananda, however, without the approval of the appropriate community leaders.

The main focus of such approval should be on the compatibility of the proposed activity with Ananda's ideals. The emphasis in this case should be positive; in other words, in the spirit of openness almost any new activity should be accepted, provided the activity doesn't contradict Ananda's ideals. For in truth, virtually any business can have a spiritual influence, if the people who serve in it do so in the consciousness of God.

MONEYS EARNED AND RECEIVED

Members have a right to keep for themselves any income they earn, or any money they receive from sources outside the community, save only such fees as all owe for the community's maintenance and improvement, for the support of the schools, etc.

Members should take it, then, not as a requirement of membership, but as natural to the spirit of cooperation and sharing, to contribute a portion of their prosperity to the welfare of all. For example, all members are expected, though not required, to tithe from their income in addition to their monthly fees, as their divine contribution to the over-all prosperity and development of their spiritual home and family. . . .

PROPERTY

No fixed property—land and buildings, in other words—may be privately owned on property that is solely held by Ananda. Members may lend, or donate, to the community a sum of money for building construction. If this sum is loaned, they have a right to be repaid, if ever they should move from that Ananda community. Members must accept repayment in terms of the community's decision as to the present value of the home. The community, for its part, has a divine duty to be fair-minded in its estimate of the value.

Traditionally, Life Member Sevakas, in a spirit and demonstration of renunciation, donate to the church any outstanding fixed-property loans or housing interest. A Life Member, in his heart at least, should offer everything he owns to God. This surrender of property rights need not mean, however, that he relinquishes stewardship of the home in which he lives. The community has the obligation to adequately house those who have donated their interest in property rights.

ACCEPTANCE OF NEW MEMBERS

The reasons for acceptance of a new member must be primarily spiritual. Considerations of his wealth, talents, or other possible contributions to the Order's welfare must always be subordinated to his spiritual qualifications.

These qualifications are simply stated: He must show sincerity in his love for God, and in his dedication to this path. Ananda's expectations of a new member are not that he be a saint, but that he enter the life at Ananda to become a saint. In accepting this way of life, it goes without saying that he should embrace all of its principles and ideals.

. . . No one should be accepted for training toward membership in the Order until he has lived at an Ananda community for at least several months. The normal initial period of training has been fixed, more by tradition than design, at two years. This time may be called a period of applicancy.

After initial training, applicants for membership may be invited to join the Ananda Monastic Order as Sevakas.

Others may choose to join the Ananda Dharmaka Order, or to become part of the broader community as Ananda Sangha members.

After a minimum of five years of additional training in the Order, Sevakas may be invited to become Sat-Sevakas or Life Members of the Order. Otherwise their acceptance may be deferred, or even mutually redefined.

MEMBERSHIP VOWS

Vows of membership in the Sevaka Order should be defined first in terms of final commitment, and then adjusted to varying degrees of commitment up to that highest level.

The final vows, then, are four: *simplicity, self-control, service,* and *cooperative obedience.*

Simplicity, at Ananda, is not defined as poverty. It is defined, rather, as reducing one's wants so that material things do not intrude on one's inner freedom, but rather, in the context of whatever needs to be done, facilitate that freedom.

Self-control means always to hold one's physical sense-pleasures in rein, and to strive to direct one's energy from the senses to soul-consciousness, rather than the reverse.

Service means less the actual activity of serving than the love one channels while serving. Indeed, for the devotee, all life should be viewed in terms of the opportunities it gives him to serve God in all.

Cooperative obedience, finally, means intelligent, creative participation in whatever one is asked to do, as opposed to that kind of obedience which asks, and is allowed to ask, no questions.

They should offer help primarily to those whom they find to be the most open to the spiritual truths that they have to share. When speaking publicly, they should invite their audiences to receive the highest that they have to give, and should not seek merely to please them. They should not hesitate to ask of others the commitment they themselves have made to the high ideals in which they believe. . . .

THE COMMUNITY AS HOME

Members should look upon Ananda as their spiritual family. They should treat community property as their own property. They should consider the interests of the members as a whole as their own interests. And they should view Ananda as their own true, spiritual home.

On a higher level of awareness, they should see their Ananda family, property, and communal interests, all, as belonging to God alone.

In God's name, above all, members should view every life form—the plants, the soil, one another, outsiders, and even those outsiders who oppose them in their way of life—with divine respect. They should consider it their duty to others of lesser vision to help to uplift, whenever they can; and, when they cannot, to bless them from afar.

For man lives on earth but a few years, but if we, as devotees of God, can live rightly, we shall live to rejoice through all eternity in Him. God-consciousness, meanwhile, remains forever our true, our only lasting home. All else is stewardship, simply, in His name.

About the Author

J. Donald Walters was born in Romania of American parents. His father was an oil geologist for Esso (Exxon), and ultimately became Esso's chief geologist for Europe. In France, years later, he was awarded the Legion of Honor.

In the present book Mr. Walters focuses a lifetime of experience on the subject of communities and their potential importance in the evolution of modern thought. Advice he often gives to other writers of philosophy is, "Persuade people by sweet reason alone. Do not pound them over the head with your credentials, nor confuse them with ungrounded logic. Let conviction come to them by recognition, based on their own experience of life."

Other Titles Available
from Crystal Clarity Publishers

Hope for a Better World
The Small Communities Solution
by Swami Kriyananda (J. Donald Walters)

In these turbulent times when wars, religious strife, stifling bureaucracy, and urban decay threaten our very humanity, reducing us to social statistics, a fresh approach to the creation of a truly viable society is desperately needed.

In this intellectual tour de force J. Donald Walters analyzes with deep insight the views expressed by many of the great thinkers in the West, including Plato, Copernicus, Machiavelli, Malthus, Adam Smith, Charles Darwin, Karl Marx, and Sigmund Freud. He studies their conceptions and misconceptions about the individual's relation to himself and to society. He shows where their influence has proved adverse, then offers deeply considered, fresh alternatives. Walters urges the reader to resist the hypnosis of "intellectual authority." Seek the key to a happy and fulfilled life, he says, in personal integrity.

Conversations with Yogananda
by Swami Kriyananda (J. Donald Walters)

This is an unparalleled, first-hand account of the teachings of Paramhansa Yogananda, author of dozens of *Autobiography of a Yogi*, who has hundreds of thousands of followers and admirers in North American alone. Featuring nearly 500 never-before-released stories, sayings, and insights, *Conversations with Yogananda* is an extensive, yet eminently accessible treasure trove of wisdom from one of the 20th Century's most famous yoga masters.

God Is for Everyone

as taught to and understood by his disciple Swami Kriyananda

Clearly and simply written, thoroughly non-sectarian and non-dogmatic in its approach, God is for Everyone is the perfect introduction to the spiritual path. Religion can offer a pragmatic, eminently useful set of solutions to our most profound problems. Importantly, this is a vision of spiritual practice that emphasizes the underlying unity of all religions, while respecting the many different ways and forms of worship. In these times of intense religious strife, this landmark approach to religious unity is certain to help usher in an era of true mutual respect and understanding among the world's great religious traditions.

Out of the Labyrinth
For Those Who Want to Believe, But Can't
J. Donald Walters

The last hundred years of scientific and philosophical thought have caused dramatic upheavals in how we view our universe, our spiritual beliefs, and ourselves. Increasingly, people are wondering if enduring spiritual and moral truths even exist.

Out of the Labyrinth brings fresh insight and understanding to this difficult problem. Walters demonstrates the genuine compatibility of scientific and religious values, and how science and our most cherished moral values actually enrich and reinforce one another. The author lays out a new approach to spirituality that both solves the problem of meaningless and champions the possibility of human transcendence and divine truth.

This book is a must for anyone struggling to find answers to these questions and the meaning of human existence.

Awaken to Superconsciousness
How to Use Meditation for Inner Peace, Intuitive Guidance, and Greater Awareness

J. Donald Walters

"A Divine guide to inner and outer peace."

—Wayne Dyer, author of *Manifest Your Destiny*

Many people have experienced moments of raised consciousness and enlightenment—or superconsciousness—but do not know how to purposely enter such an exalted state. Superconsciousness is the hidden mechanism at work behind intuition, spiritual and physical healing, successful problem solving, and finding deep, lasting joy.

Through meditation, chanting, affirmation, and prayer, readers will learn how to reach this state successfully and regularly and how to maximize its beneficial effects. Awaken to Superconsciousness provides a comprehensive, easy-to-understand routine to help people tap into their wellspring of creativity, unlock intuitive guidance, and hear the silent voice of their soul.

Crystal Clarity Publishers

For a free catalog or to place an order, please call:
800.424.1055 or 530.478.7600
fax. 530.478.7610
clarity@crystalclarity.com
www.crystalclarity.com